ON DUTIES

A Guide To Conduct, Obligations, And Decision-Making

By

Marcus Tullius Cicero

A New Annotated Translation
With Notes, Commentary And Index

By

Quintus Curtius

ON DUTIES
Copyright © 2016 by Quintus Curtius
All rights reserved.

Cover design by massurrealist artist James Seehafer

Printed in the United States of America

Published by Fortress of the Mind Publications™
qcurtius.com

ISBN-13: 978-1534802254
ISBN-10: 1534802258

For my parents

TABLE OF CONTENTS

PREFACE

On Duties (*De officiis*) may be the most famous of Cicero's many philosophical works. After the Gutenberg Bible, it was apparently the first printed book published in Europe upon the advent of the printing press. Voltaire, in his *Philosophical Dictionary* of 1764, said of it that "no one will ever write anything more wise." And Voltaire was not one to give out praise easily. The Prussian king Frederick the Great commissioned his own German translation, and read the work with great care.[1] The large number of surviving manuscripts (around seven hundred) attests to its enduring popularity in the Middle Ages and during the Renaissance.

It is not difficult to see why the book has enjoyed such influence. *On Duties* is a very practical guide to conduct, responsibilities, and choices. Cicero defines his terms, makes his arguments, and illustrates his points with a wealth of examples. We are never for a moment led into an arid wilderness of metaphysics or gratuitous speculations. Written at a time of great personal anguish for Cicero, the book has a sincerity and forthrightness that draws us in from the opening chapters. The reader feels that Cicero is a man who has learned much from the battlefields of politics, the courtroom, and personal relations; we sense that this is a man who has managed to maintain his moral compass, and who now wishes to pass on some of that wisdom to us.

---

[1] Theodor Schieder, *Frederick the Great*, New York: Routledge, 2013, p. 245.

Despite the book's popularity and influence, there has long been a need for a new, annotated translation of this classic. What may have sufficed for one century or generation may be found wanting for twenty-first century readers. Hence this work. The present translation departs from its predecessors in three important respects. First, most of the existing English translations were done many years ago. Such efforts, which may have been adequate for their era, unavoidably begin to show their age after a certain point. The modern reader wants something accurate and readable, yet which at the same time preserves the classic patina of the original. Unfortunately, some of the existing translations confront the reader with such a hopeless mass of semi-colons, stacked clauses, archaic nineteenth century diction, and knotted sentences that reading them is a chore rather than a pleasure. Cicero was an eloquent stylist, always conscious of his audience, and a faithful translation should strive to do justice to the original.

We must remember that Cicero was *always* the lawyer, arguing his points with force, conviction, and clarity. When he repeats himself, he does so deliberately. When he castigates political opponents, he does so for a reason. When he tells us multiple times that nothing can be expedient which is not also morally good, he does so deliberately. These are not accidents. He knows that juries, like book readers, need emotional connection, summary and repetition. Some translators, because they are not trial attorneys by profession, entirely miss this point.

But those of us who have tried cases before juries—and I am not aware of any other translator of *On Duties* who was also a trial lawyer—see the method and purpose in Cicero's rhetoric. But the translator must not veer to the other extreme: while Cicero did not write like a Victorian or Edwardian novelist, he did not sound like Chuck Palahniuk, either. A good translation should still be redolent of its period. We should not only understand the text; we should also be brought back to its era. So when we seek to translate *On Duties* for the modern reader, we must go about the task very carefully, keeping these points in mind. The needs of modern pedagogy must not be permitted to suffocate the author's words or the spirit of the original.

In a previous translation of one of Cicero's works (*Stoic Paradoxes*), I briefly discussed some of the challenges faced by his translators. The text of *On Duties* is generally clear. Some of Cicero's sentences are long, with multiple ideas and clauses following each other in close sequence. In these situations, aiming for a robotic one-for-one equivalence in English would be reckless and irresponsible. As I see it, the most important duty of the translator is to find that delicate balance between fidelity to the original text and the stylistic rhythms of modern written English. Every language beats with its own heart, and the translator must keep his fingers carefully on the pulses of both the original and the target idiom.

What may make perfect sense in a Latin sentence may be anything but clear in a literal English rendering. The creative translator must use the available English grammatical tools to give Cicero his proper voice. Labyrinthine sentences may occasionally need to be broken into parts. Latin pronouns may need to be specifically clarified. Cicero's love of the passive voice must sometimes be tempered with use of the active voice. We must know when Cicero really means "I" when he writes "we." He can be evasive and slithery one moment, and brutally frank at another. At times, his meaning resides in his qualifications and obliquities. And so on. Modern, lucid diction should be the translator's default position, unless the context clearly suggests otherwise, as when Cicero quotes the antique poet Ennius.

Secondly, it became apparent that a much better way of organizing the material was needed. *On Duties* deals with a great many topics and terms. Like all classical writings, the text long ago was separated into "books," chapters, and subsections by scribes and editors; but Cicero never gave his chapters descriptive headings or names. Locating a topic or term easily can then present a problem. Some editors have made use of marginal notes, but these tend to clutter the text, and still require the reader to thumb through too many pages. I have thus opted to create a descriptive table of contents at the beginning of the book which lists the main topics of each chapter (indicated by Roman numerals). This feature, together with the index, solves the problem of locating subjects and topics efficiently. This is a book that is meant not only to be read, studied, and discussed, but also to be used.

Thirdly, the modern reader requires descriptive footnotes that presume no previous knowledge of Roman history. A translator can no longer take it for granted that a reader in 2016 will recognize, for example, the names Regulus or Titus Manlius Torquatus. As stated above, most versions of *On Duties* were produced for audiences in the previous century who were assumed to have some knowledge of Roman history or Latin, and likely both. This translation presupposes no such knowledge. It is accessible to all, not just to students of the classics.

Two hundred fifty-six footnotes explain every historical name and reference, as well as obscure terms, linguistic nuances, places, topics, or textual issues. In the Kindle version of this book, readers can click on the footnote number in the text to be brought to the footnote itself. And while it is intended for the general reader, this book also provides enough rigorous detail to meet the needs of the serious student.

For these reasons, I believe the present translation is the most complete and readable version of *On Duties* available in English.

Quintus Curtius
April 2016

INTRODUCTION

It is likely that Cicero composed *On Duties* midway through the year in 44.[2] We have several clues that point to this conclusion. The assassination of Julius Caesar is alluded to in the text itself as a recent incident. Cicero's statements to his son Marcus give the impression that he wrote the treatise soon after Marcus arrived in Athens to study under the philosopher Cratippus. One of Cicero's letters to his friend Atticus (XV.15) indicates that Marcus had gone to Athens in the early spring of 45. It would be reasonable to assume, then, a composition time of early summer in 44.

Cicero had a long and sincere interest in philosophy, as the biographical sketch in the following pages will show. But as he points out at the beginning of book II (II.1), he did not have much time for it when he was absorbed in his career as a lawyer and politician. He was trying cases, advocating for clients, and getting himself involved (or entangled) in the exhilarating but dangerous political affairs of his day. It was indeed a turbulent era. The old republic was dying, its institutions stretched to their limits by factionalism, the greed of the wealthy classes, and the unchecked ambition of powerful personalities. Cicero picked the wrong side in the conflict between Caesar and Pompey, but might have reconciled himself to Caesar's new order had Caesar not been

---

[2] Hereafter dates will be "B.C." unless otherwise noted. When referring to the text of *On Duties*, we will use the convention of book (in Roman numerals), followed by chapter (in Arabic numerals), then subsection (also in Arabic numerals).

tragically assassinated. His death unleased a fury of retribution by Antony and Octavian that made a point of hunting down anyone who had opposed Caesar in the past. The senate and law courts were inactive or closed, and Cicero had little to do except write. But his misfortune turned out to be our blessing. For in a short period of time, he turned out a large number of philosophical works. The best and most famous of these works is *On Duties*. Let us now examine it in some detail.

His candid purpose is to provide ethical guidance to his twenty-year-old son Marcus. He was born in 65, and Cicero devoted significant resources to his training and education. Cicero brought Marcus with him when he traveled in Greece and Asia Minor in 51. Later, during the civil war, he secured for his son a position under Pompey's command. Marcus would eventually see some modest success in political office; and after the elder Cicero was slain on Antony's orders, Marcus naturally became an ally and associate of Octavian. After the defeat and suicide of Antony, Octavian appointed Marcus proconsul of Syria and Asia. After this we hear nothing more of him. Perhaps, having witnessed the fate of his father, he thought it better to live the remainder of his life as a private citizen. If so, he at least had the satisfaction of participating in Antony's downfall and witnessing the revocation of his honors.

We should mention a few important points about the contents and terminology of *On Duties*. The text is separated into three books. The first book deals with the nature of "moral goodness" or "moral rectitude" (*honestas, honestum*). The second book is concerned with issues of moral "advantageousness" or "expediency" (*utilis, utilitas*). The third and final book discusses how to resolve conflicts between these two apparent opposites.[3] A wealth of examples are deployed in support of his arguments:

---

[3] To emphasize this "conflict," Cicero uses the verbs *pugnare* or *contendere*, which give his tone an emphatic one.

he borrows freely from Greek and Roman history, as well as from his own experience in politics. Cicero here and there refers to the philosopher Panaetius's lost treatise on moral duties, and seems to have been inspired at least in part by reading it.

There are some surprises here as well. He gives us an admirable review of commercial contract law, the law of war, even real estate transactions; he even finds space to talk about the art of conversation, decorum, and the need to avoid lewd conduct. He takes great care to remind us repeatedly that nothing can be expedient that is not also morally good, and that even if things appear to be otherwise, they are not.

But perhaps what elevates *On Duties* to true greatness is its soaring and inspiring vision of man. This is no dry collection of Poor Richard-esque admonitions to do good and shun evil; this is a normative vision of human behavior that seeks to bring out the very best in us. Man, he explains, was created by Nature and endowed with reason; he is different from other animals, and has an obligation to unite himself with his fellows in bonds of trust, cooperation, and goodwill (I.4). He achieves true profundity when he tells us (II.7) that the bonds of love are more enduring than those forged by fear. Perhaps his grandest concept—one that lingers in the mind of the reader long after he has closed the cover of the book—is the idea of "greatness of spirit" (*magnitudo animi*). Cicero gives us an idea of what he means by greatness of spirit in I.20 when he tells us:

A strong and great soul is altogether distinguished by two features. One is the contempt for the external things of this world. The great soul is persuaded that no man ought to wonder at, hope for, or seek after anything except those things related to goodness and virtue, and that he should succumb to neither another man, nor a disturbance of the spirit, nor a trial of Fortune. The second feature is that, when you have molded your soul with this sort of attitude, as I said above, you perform great achievements of the highest utility which are extremely arduous, laborious, and full of danger to life and to many other things related to one's livelihood.

With his concept of *magnitudo animi*, Cicero thus takes the discussion to a whole other level. What we have here is an inspiring vision of man, something that penetrates the reader's heart like an arrow. This, I believe, is the essential thread running through the book. It is this which makes *On Duties* such an enduring treasure.

His sincere, earnest vision is timeless, and this is why we still read him today. This is the spirit that I have tried to capture in this translation, and it is this spirit that I hope the reader will savor in the pages that follow. For Cicero's purpose is not simply to rattle off the characteristics of moral goodness and expediency; he realizes that no dry enumeration of rights and wrongs will captivate the minds of his readers. Like any great orator (and was there anyone greater?) he aims far higher, for more universal and evocative principles. And he succeeds brilliantly. When we put down *On Duties*, we feel imbued by this same greatness of spirit, and are prepared to renew the contest of life with optimism and fortitude.

It remains only for me to thank those who helped bring this project to fruition. Especially worthy of mention are my friend and editor, Winston Smith, for his many textual suggestions and comments. I am also very grateful for the consistent and enthusiastic support provided by Zeljko Ivić over a long period of time. Zeljko is a true gentleman, and his sensitivity and scholarly impulses have never ceased to amaze me. The massurrealist artist James Seehafer also deserves special mention for his inspired cover design that captures perfectly the spirit of the work. I am privileged and humbled that an artist of James's renown was able to contribute to the project. Gratitude is also owed to my father for patiently reviewing the entire manuscript and offering his own valued suggestions. For any imperfections that may still lurk in these pages, of course, I assume sole responsibility.

The Latin text of *On Duties* used in this translation was that of *M. Tullii Ciceronis de officiis libri tres*, New York: Hinds, Noble & Eldredge, 3rd ed., 1910.

THE LIFE OF CICERO

We know more about Marcus Tullius Cicero than nearly any other figure of Roman antiquity. His vanity has worked to our advantage, for never has a man taken such care to write so much about himself. He carefully transcribed and published his political speeches; he wrote numerous philosophical works; and his private correspondence, likely never intended for publication, gives us a taste of the workings of his mind, and the mood of the era. He has had his detractors through the centuries, and remains a controversial figure; but his contradictions of personality continue to make him a fascinating object for study.

Kind, generous, sensitive, loyal, idealistic, and at times brave, he could also be hypocritical, arrogant, boorish, and egotistical to a fault. He had the misfortune of living at a time of severe political turbulence, where the old social systems and forms of governance were crumbling before the weight of Rome's expanding empire and rigid class structure. His ultimate failure as a political leader may be traced to his inability to appreciate (unlike his contemporary Julius Caesar) the fact that the old republic needed to be drastically reformed to meet the challenges of Rome's new position as a global power.

And yet, despite Cicero's limited political vision, he remains perhaps the most influential of all his peers. His name is rightly synonymous with eloquence. Although he considered himself most significant as an attorney and politician, it is ironic that his enduring fame has come from his reputation as a man of letters. His philosophical works, composed at incredible speed in the span of only two or three years, are gems of moral guidance. He never claimed to be an entirely original thinker, but achieved a brand of originality nonetheless by bringing the monuments of Greek philosophy to the Latin-speaking world. He created, nearly single-handedly, an entire vocabulary of philosophical terms in Latin, and managed to popularize the key tenets of Greek thought.

St. Augustine credited him with firing his imagination with a love for philosophy; the Renaissance humanist Poggio Bracciolini loved him so much that he wrote letters to him, as if he were still alive; and Erasmus considered him to be nearly without peer.[4] The Middle Ages and the Renaissance worshipped him, and held him almost to be an honorary Christian. His influence over European literature was so immense that imitation of his writing style was held out as an unquestioned normative standard for many centuries. If we are to understand the man, we must examine his life and times. Let us now turn to the man, and see what we may find.

He was born in 106 B.C. near the small town of Arpinum (modern Arpino), at roughly a midway point between Rome and Naples.[5] The town is about seventy miles east of Rome. He came from an equestrian family which was rich enough, but not too rich.[6] His father had that key virtue of paternity, which is the exertion of all efforts to see that his children received the best education possible. Cicero was tutored in Greek, and then studied rhetoric and law with Quintus Mucius Scaevola, who was one of the most influential legal figures of his day. At the age of about seventeen he served for a brief period in the army. It was at an

---

[4] See, e.g., Augustine's *Confessions* III.5-9 for the story of his exposure to Cicero's *Hortensius*.

[5] Cicero speaks of his upbringing in Arpinum in *De legibus* II.1.3: *Quia, si verum dicimus, haec est mea et huius fratris mei germana patria; hic enim orti stirpe antiquissima sumus, hic sacra, hic genus, hic maiorum multa vestigia. Quid plura?*

[6] The equestrian order (called *equites*, or sometimes "knights") was the lower of the two aristocratic classes of the Roman republic. The class above the *equites* was the patricians.

early age that Cicero began to display the astonishing facility with speech-making and verbal sparring that would prove to be so important in his later life. It was not long before his ability to argue cases won him notoriety and an abundance of clients.

On the darker side of things, it must be said that in these early years Cicero also displayed a character trait that would haunt him throughout his life, and contribute to his ultimate downfall: an inability to know when to be silent in the face of injustices committed by men far more ruthless than he was. For he was living in perilous times. The strains caused by Rome's expanding dominion around the Mediterranean had caused severe social problems in Italy. Wealth and power had become too concentrated in the hands of a few, who were unwilling to share it with those below them in the social layer cake. Ambitious generals, taking advantage of the social paralysis, capitalized on the frustrations of disenfranchised youths, plebs, and debtors unable or unwilling to earn their bread by labor.

One of these generals was a man named Sulla. He had come from a very modest background to lead a large following of troops who were more loyal to him personally than to the Senate. When he wanted to be, he was a charming man, but he was also a violent and ruthless one who craved power and did not care much how he got it. In the year 88 he led his army into Rome, in what would today be called a coup. His opponents were slain or exiled. Sulla then departed for the east to make war on Mithradates and expand Rome's domain. Seeing an opportunity in his absence, other ambitious men (Cinna and Marius) tried to take power in Rome. Cinna managed to hold Italy for a few years until Sulla returned in 83 to take a bloody vengeance. He defeated Cinna, became sole dictator, and proscribed (i.e., killed) vast numbers of Cinna's supporters, both real and imaginary. For years Rome lived in an atmosphere of fear and repression. On the other hand, Sulla did leave voluntarily in 79, after having written a new republican constitution.

It is beyond question that the memory of these violent events left a strong impression on the young Cicero. As the armies of warring factions staggered up and down the Italian peninsula, he would have watched with a mixture of apprehension and fascination. He was not naturally inclined to be a man of action; his battles were fought in the law-courts and with his stylus. But at the same time, he was a man of order, and hated the spectacle of generals trampling on the sacred institutions of the republic. The regimes of both Cinna and Sulla stirred his contempt. He had a sharp tongue, and he knew how to use it. It would not be long before he would find himself in trouble with those in power.

And so it was that in 80 he undertook to defend a man named Roscius, who was being maligned by a crony of Sulla. He not only defended Roscius, but went on the offensive against Sulla's apparatus of repression by denouncing the proscriptions. This was brave, but unwise. Dictators are not known for forgiving or forgetting a slight, especially when the insult comes from a man with no legions. Thus Cicero found it expedient to leave Rome for a period of time. For three years he studied philosophy and rhetoric in Greece and Asia Minor. He attended the lectures on rhetoric of Apollonius Molon on the island of Rhodes, and those of Posidonius on Stoicism. Both of these men were celebrated figures. This sabbatical was a happy period for him; he was able to polish his mastery of the Greek language, expose himself to new philosophical doctrines, and plan the future trajectory of his career.

He found himself back in Rome after his sojourn in Greece, and from that point devoted himself completely to law and politics. At the age of thirty he married Terentia, a woman of likely patrician stock who provided Cicero the financial boost and connections needed to be a competitor in Roman politics. He enjoyed many years of domestic felicity with her, but financial troubles brought on by Cicero's political tribulations ultimately doomed their marriage, and they divorced in 46. But that heartache was for the future. Beginning in 75, he had many years of successes, including being elected to several offices at the earliest age that candidacy was possible. First came a successful quaestorship in Sicily; when this ended he was hired by several Sicilian municipalities to prosecute a corrupt official named Caius Verres.

Verres had enriched himself with bribes and plundered the region he had been appointed to administer, and the business classes wanted his head. Cicero gave it to them. He methodically collected evidence against Verres, and demolished him in his opening statement at trial; the damage was so severe that Verres's attorney, Hortensius, immediately conceded defeat. Cicero published the remaining Verrine speeches, although none were actually delivered; they remain nearly unmatched as examples of pure invective.

He ran for, and was elected to, the position of consul in 63. This was a major achievement, for the consulship in those days was normally reserved for the nobility and Cicero was not of aristocratic background. As we have previously noted, his family was of comfortable middle-class (equestrian) origin. He would have been considered by his patrician allies as a *novus homo* ("new man"); that is, a man lacking in ancient patrician lineage. As basically a self-made man, Cicero privately had little respect for aristocrats and their pretensions; yet he despised even more the rabble-rousing and demagoguery of popular orators who sought to overthrow the established order.

Cicero's greatest moment of political attention came in suppressing the so-called "conspiracy of Catiline" in 65-64. Lucius Sergius Catiline was a patrician politician who appears to have been one of the many unscrupulous figures of the era who sought to gain power by force rather than by persuasion. He left nothing in writing; we know of him only through the accounts of his enemies, the implacable Cicero and the brilliant historian

Sallust.[7] But this is damaging enough, even if we make the appropriate discounts for partisanship. Catiline, with the help of some marginalized and dispossessed followers, had planned on seizing power and cancelling all debts for those unable to pay. According to Sallust and Cicero, Catiline's plan was to murder key figures of the government (including Cicero himself) in 65, cancel all debts, and then embark on a program of wide-ranging reforms.

Cicero discovered the plot, and destroyed Catiline's position in a series of scorching speeches. These four speeches are his most famous orations, and remain among the best examples of pure vituperation ever delivered. It is generally conceded now that Cicero's unmasking of the plot saved the republic from years of strife; but he did not emerge from the affair unscathed, for he had ordered the execution without trial of several aristocratic henchmen of Catiline. This did not sit well with the Roman power structure. Despite their complicity, the conspirators were Roman citizens and were guaranteed the right to a trial.

In the Catilinian speeches themselves, we can catch glimpses of Cicero's complex personality: fiercely protective of republican institutions, yet perhaps secretly resentful of Catiline's patrician upbringing. Some patricians (including Julius Caesar) argued against the death penalty for the adherents of Catiline, but they were overruled; Cicero had his way, and personally oversaw the executions. His prestige was at its height, and he was hailed as *pater patriae* ("father of his country") by Cato and a few other conservatives, but Romans would soon grow tired of hearing from him about how he had saved them from anarchy. Cicero had his moment of glory, but the republic was suffering from a terminal illness. Catiline was just the symptom of a deeper problem that

---

[7] His *Bellum Catilinae* (The War of Catiline) remains a masterpiece of historiography and rhetoric.

remained unsolved: the unequal distribution of wealth, the lack of land reform, and the failure of the political system to respond to the needs of an expanding population and empire.

After the Catilinian affair, the duel between Caesar and Pompey and its aftermath would occupy Cicero's attention. The cracks in the republican edifice could no longer be plastered over; the social issues would now be settled by armed conflict. The contest between these two men, fought across Italy and the Mediterranean, was a true civil war, and would put the final nails in the coffin of the republic. In many ways Cicero lacked political vision, and was wedded to a conception of the republic that had already passed into history. For all his incredible skill as an attorney, an advocate, and as a writer, he failed to comprehend the seismic changes that were taking place in the Roman world before his very eyes. This fact would contribute to his tragic downfall.

Julius Caesar became consul in 59, but Cicero disliked him and distrusted his populist leanings. Worse still, Caesar was suspected of having had secret sympathies for the Catilinian conspirators. Caesar tried to woo him, but Cicero was not interested; he leaned towards Caesar's rival Pompey. But there were other sharks in the water as well. Cicero was outmaneuvered and forced into exile in Greece in 58 by a conniving politician named Publius Clodius Pulcher, but was able to return eighteen months later.[8] For a time Cicero tried to play the factions of Caesar and Pompey against each other, but he was an amateur in a game for which he was ill-suited.

At some point Cicero recognized the inevitable rise of Caesar and reached an accommodation with him; probably at Cicero's suggestion, his brother Quintus went to Gaul to serve in the military, where Caesar was making history with his subjugation

---

[8] Clodius is believed to have been the unnamed target in Paradoxes II and IV in Cicero's *Stoic Paradoxes*.

of the country. In 51, Cicero served as governor of the province of Cilicia in Asia Minor, a geographical division that included the island of Cyprus.

When open warfare broke out between Caesar and Pompey in 49, Cicero was faced with the prospect of having to choose sides. Pompey's death in 48 after the Battle of Pharsalia simplified things; as a victor Caesar was of legendary leniency, and Cicero could finally, so he believed, find some measure of relief from political intrigue. He devoted himself almost entirely to writing philosophy during these fretful years. The death of his daughter Tullia in February 45 was a major shock to him. Depression immobilized him for a time, but his literary projects seem to have revived him.

Being now a political museum piece, Cicero spent his time at his country estates, writing and receiving visitors. He played no part in the conspiracy which took Caesar's life in 44, but he certainly endorsed the murder of the dictator as necessary (so he believed) for the restoration of the old republican order. The conspirator Brutus had been a close personal friend of his. What Cicero could never understand was that the republic had been doomed long before the advent of Caesar. Caesar had not destroyed it; it had been destroyed from within by the failure of the patrician class to promote meaningful reforms of the political and economic order. Cicero may have been a competent political tactician, but he was incapable of appreciating the larger historical trends that were influencing the events of the day.

Cicero, like the conspirators who murdered Caesar, had not counted on the ruthlessness and resiliency of Mark Antony, who quickly emerged as another aspiring dictator. Exhausted from years of double-dealing, intrigue, and violent spectacles, he now threw caution to the wind and committed the blunder that sealed his fate.

It is ironic that, at the end of his political career, Cicero would commit an act so similar to what he did at the beginning of his career when he spoke out against the dictator Sulla's repression. But a man's character determines his fate; and for better or for worse, Cicero was unable to hold his tongue when he saw something that outraged him. Perhaps there was some secret self-destructive impulse that drove him forward. So from 44 to 43, he delivered a series of brilliant speeches against Antony in the Senate, which he called *Philippics* in honor of his hero, the Greek orator Demosthenes.[9] At the same time, the wily Cicero tried to ingratiate himself with the young Octavian, whom he believed could serve as a counterweight to Antony.

His popularity achieved new heights, and he began to organize supporters to resist Antony, whom he believed was a serious danger to the republic. But here again, Cicero showed himself to be a poor judge of character where it counted, for he misread both Antony and Octavian. He seriously underestimated the ambition and resourcefulness of the former, and totally discounted the patient ability of the latter. These omissions would prove to be fatal.

The drama of Cicero's life had one final act remaining. An incredibly young Octavian occupied Rome and assumed power. Octavian, Antony, and fellow triumvir Lepidus agreed to act jointly to secure power. First on the order of business was to take vengeance on anyone who had supported the assassination of Caesar. Antony had neither forgiven nor forgotten Cicero's Philippics; and Octavian, as Caesar's adopted son and heir, acquiesced in the decision to have Cicero killed. And so it was that the great orator became a hunted man. He remained popular with the common people, but everyone knew that a new regime was now in control, and that defiance to it could bring retribution on anyone's head.

---

[9] Demosthenes had called his own speeches against Philip of Macedon "Philippics." By borrowing the name from his predecessor, Cicero was implicitly equating himself with him. But he probably exceeded his predecessor in eloquence.

On December 7 in 43, a party of soldiers apprehended him as he was about to escape by sea to Macedonia. He was being carried in a litter, and it is said that one of his slaves betrayed his identity to the assassins. According to Plutarch, Cicero did not resist death; he leaned his head out of his litter, presented his neck to the gladius of his executioner, and stoically accepted his fate. His last words were, "What you are doing is not right, soldier, but do try to dispatch me correctly." He was decapitated, and his hands were then amputated; these grisly trophies the vindictive Antony caused to be displayed publicly in Rostra of the Forum. It was a bitter and tragic end to a man of flawed, but towering, genius. His brother Quintus was also hunted down and executed.

Cicero had the faults that his abilities created. We miss in him the broad vision and patient maturity of Caesar. He cared about the mentorship of the young, and took his profession very seriously as a form of service to his country; but he also could be self-serving, vain and politically myopic. Perhaps so; but in these things he was not alone. In many ways there was an honest consistency to his political career: he never wavered in his belief that the republic must be preserved and protected. In one letter to his friend Atticus, he confides his sorrow at seeing the collapse of the republic he tried to save:

> I am sustained by a clear conscience, as I believe I was able to provide the republic with the best of my ability, and I never wavered from loyalty to it. And this same tempest that has rocked the republic was predicted by me fourteen years ago. And so I go forward with this conscience as my companion, and certainly with great sadness; not for my sake or the sake of my brother, since we have had our time, but for the sake of our boys, who as I see it deserved to have a real republic...[10]

---

[10] *Letters to Atticus*, X.4.5 (Letter 195).

If he held on too tightly to the past in his political beliefs, it was because he could see nothing but chaos resulting from the dismantling of republican institutions. And if, when reading his speeches today in books far removed from their period and context, we feel him to be at times an apostle of invective, we must remember that Cicero was speaking to a Mediterranean audience that expected high drama and histrionic verbosity from its orators. We must always be careful to separate the public from the private Cicero. The private man—so different from the public persona he adopted to protect himself in shark-filled political waters—was learned, scholarly, honest, even profoundly spiritual. And which of us today, if our private correspondence were revealed for all the world (as was Cicero's in his voluminous letters to his friend Atticus and others), would emerge with our reputations unscathed?

Much of the self-praise he heaped on himself derived from an inner insecurity that Cicero acquired early in his career and never shook off. He remained forever the *novus homo*, the "new man," in a world of landed patricians who never let him forget where he had come from. Cicero's ultimate mistake was in believing he could play the game of Roman politics with characters who far surpassed him in chicanery. He remains essentially a tragic figure; a man who believed he was acting in the best interests of his country, but was hamstrung by his own flawed personality and the perilous times in which he lived.

And yet, despite all this, his political career is the least important part of his legacy to the world. No one today much worries about Cicero's reputation as a politician. His writings give him immortality. It is ironic that Cicero has emerged as the most influential of all his contemporaries by far, with the possible exception of Julius Caesar.

If we define influence as the impact on the lives of people, Cicero is nearly unchallenged. It was he who imported Greek philosophy to the Roman world, and made it digestible to his countrymen. It was he who coined new words, concepts, phrases, and terms in Latin. He shaped and molded the Latin language as no man before or after him, so that it would be able to convey the most subtle and complex philosophical ideas. He was studied, imitated, and worshipped for centuries as a paragon of Latin style, and as a philosopher of the highest rank. The wily old lawyer may have had the last word after all.

Plutarch closes his *Life of Cicero* with this anecdote, which sums up his subject's epitaph as well as any could:

> A long time afterwards, so I have been told, [Julius] Caesar was writing to one of his daughter's sons. The boy had a book of Cicero's in his hands and, terrified of his grandfather, tried to hide it under his cloak. Caesar noticed this and, after taking the book from him, stood there and read a great part of it. He then handed it back to the young man with these words: "A learned man, my child, a learned man and a lover of his country."[11]

---

[11] *Life of Cicero*, 49. See *Plutarch: Fall of the Roman Republic*, London: Penguin Books, 2005, p. 373.

BOOK I: THE NATURE OF MORAL GOODNESS

Book I

I. [1] Marcus, my son, since you have been attending the lectures of Cratippus for a year now in Athens, you ought to be well-instructed in the doctrines and fundamentals of philosophy, due to both the eminence of your teacher and the renown of the city.[12] One of these adds to your theoretical knowledge, and the other to your practical skills. Nevertheless, from my own experience, I have fruitfully joined Greek and Latin studies not only in philosophy, but in oratorical training; and I believe you should do the same, so that you achieve facility in speaking in both languages. In this regard we may indeed be seen has having rendered a great service to our people, so that not only those who are unschooled in Greek letters, but also the educated elite, may believe they have acquired the arts of speaking and critical thinking.

[2] For this reason, you are learning from the most well-known philosophers of our era. And you will continue to learn as you wish. You ought to desire this, and will not regret it as long as you continue to advance. Still, as you read, you will see that we do not differ much from the Peripatetics, as we both wish to be aligned with the Socratics and Platonists. In these matters you must use your own judgment (I will certainly not influence you); but you will accomplish much more in Latin rhetoric by reading

---

[12] Cratippus of Pergamon was an Aristotelian (Peripatetic) philosopher and lived for a time at Mitylene. Cicero actually met him once on his way to the governorship of Cilicia. Caesar conferred citizenship on Cratippus at Cicero's request.

my writings. I would not wish you to think that this is something said arrogantly. Conceding to many others' knowledge of philosophy, I believe I myself can claim the mantle of the orator, which is the ability to speak correctly, distinctly, and lucidly, since I have devoted my career to this subject.

[3] So for this reason, my dear Cicero, I earnestly request that you read not only my orations, but also my books on philosophy (which number about the same amount). The orations as a class are more forceful in language; but temperance of style must equally be cultivated. I see no one among the Greeks with the ability to have combined these two things, to the extent that he can elaborate and correctly follow both the precepts of forensic speaking and nuanced philosophical speculation, except perhaps Demetrius of Phalerum, who may be such a man. He is a subtle debater, an orator lacking in power, but still pleasant, so that you can identify him as a student of Theophrastus.[13] It may be the judgment of others how much I have advanced in each of these fields.[14] I have certainly tried my hand at both.

[4] I equally believe that if Plato had wanted to practice forensic oratory, he could have spoken most wonderfully and with power; and I also believe that if Demosthenes, since he had learned from Plato, had wanted to advocate Plato's views, he could have done so with elegance and resonance.[15] I judge Aristotle and Isocrates the same way. Each one was perfectly charmed by his own activity, and thus disparaged the other.

II. Now since I have decided to write something to you at this time, and many more things later, I want to begin earnestly with

---

[13] Demetrius of Phalerum (c.350-280 B.C.) was one of the last great Attic orators, and was known for his elegant rhetorical style. He is featured in Diogenes Laertius's *Lives of the Philosophers*.

[14] I.e., in forensic oratory and philosophical speculation.

[15] Forensic rhetoric (as distinguished from deliberative rhetoric and epideictic rhetoric) focused on discussions of past actions or legal issues.

topics most suited to your age, and most suited to my experience. Since many serious and useful things are disputed in philosophy—accurately and at great length—by philosophers, the principles which have been passed down from these men are properly seen to have the widest utility. In no part of life, whether in public, in private, in business affairs or in the household, whether you do something alone or enter into some agreement with another, can one be free of moral duties. In the cultivation of this duty in life are found all things honest, and in the neglect of this responsibility are all things morally wrong.

[5] And indeed this question is a common one among all philosophers. Who would dare call himself a philosopher, who proposes no general precepts of moral duty? But there are a few schools, which through their ideas on the nature of good and evil, significantly distort the idea of duty. He who proposes the idea of the "highest good" in such a way that it is completely disconnected with moral virtue, and rather measures it according to how it relates to one's personal expediency (if he felt this way, and were not governed by his better nature), can cultivate neither friendship, nor justice, nor generosity. He who judges pain to be the greatest evil is certainly in no way strong; and he who sets up pleasure as the highest good cannot be considered temperate.

[6] Although these matters are readily obvious, such that further discussion is not necessary, they have been argued elsewhere. If these philosophical schools wish to be agreeable, they may say nothing about duty. No firm, stable, and natural principles of moral duty can be described except by those who say that it must be sought for the sake of moral goodness alone. This doctrine is a specialty of the Stoics, Academics, and Peripatetics, since the theories of Aristo, Pyrrho and Erillus have long since

been rejected.[16] They nevertheless might have the right to discuss duties if they had left us the ability to select[17] things, so that one might find a way of discovering what duty is. We will follow most usefully here at this time, and in these questions, the Stoics. We follow them not as messengers; but we will draw from them in such amount and in such a way as our judgment and consideration may deem necessary.

[7] It will be useful at this point to specify *what is moral duty*, since our entire discussion will be about it. I am surprised that this definition was omitted by Panaetius.[18] Everything that is taken up by reason for learned discussion ought to begin with definitions, so that the object of discussion may be properly understood, and all may know what arguments are being made.

III. There are two questions in discussions on duty. One question is: *what is related to the "ultimate good" and its purposes*? The other question is: *what general rules can be laid out by which one's life may be shaped*? These are examples of the first type of question: whether all moral duties are complete in themselves, whether one moral duty is greater than another, and what are the various categories of these duties. As for the duties for which general precepts are proposed, although these are

---

[16] Aristo of Chios (fl. 260 B.C.) was a student of Zeno and the founder of his own school. Pyrrho of Elis was a Skeptic who flourished near the end of the fourth century B.C. Erillus was a Carthaginian student of Zeno. Aristo and Pyrrho apparently believed that virtue was the only good; Erillus believed that knowledge was also co-equal to virtue as a good. But they also believed that man, with his imperfect senses and uncertain judgments, was incapable of evaluating the truth or falsity of anything. Cicero rejected this sort of wish-washy indeterminism.

[17] I read here *delectum*, and not *dilectum*.

[18] Panaetius of Rhodes (c.185—110 B.C.) was a Stoic philosopher greatly re-spected by Cicero. He was an eclectic in philosophical matters, and borrowed freely from other schools. He wrote a treatise on moral duties in three books, and this seems partly to have been the inspiration for Cicero's own book.

related to knowledge of the "ultimate good," nevertheless it is less obvious, because they seem to deal with the rules of everyday life. The explication of these duties is our task in the books that follow here.

There is, in addition, another type of moral duty.

[8] There can be said to be the "medium" duty and the "perfect" duty. We may call perfect duty "right duty," I think, since this term in Greek is *katorthoma*; common duty is termed *kathekon*. The Greeks define these terms in this way. If something may be a "right duty," they define it to be "perfect duty." If, however, they state that something is a "medium duty," they mean that we can infer a probable reason for why the duty may have been carried out.

[9] As Panaetius informed us, there are three deliberations involved in reaching a decision. When people think about whether to do something, they are uncertain if it may be a morally good deed or an immoral one. In pondering this, they are often distracted by many contrary sentiments. Then they inquire and deliberate whether the action is profitable and pleasurable for their lives, whether it gives them power and wealth, or resources or influence, which may be able to help them and their comrades. This deliberation looks at everything from the viewpoint of utilitarian reasoning. The third type of deliberation arises when that which is *morally good* is seen to conflict with that which is *expedient*. As expediency is seen to pull a man in one direction, and moral rectitude calls him in another, the result is that his mind is distracted in deliberation. Thinking thus promotes the anxiety of indecision.

[10] In this division (although passing over something in the above classification is a big defect), two things have been omitted. We are not only used to considering whether something is morally right or wrong, but also, when weighing two honest propositions, which of those is the most honest. In the same way, when deliberating on two expedient propositions, we are used to

selecting which one has greater utility. Thus, although he[19] first thought there were three considerations, we really find that there ought to be five.

First, therefore, we must discuss issues involving moral goodness, but in a two-fold fashion. Then we must discuss with equal consideration those issues involving expediency. Finally, we will compare them.

IV. [11] It is a principle of Nature granted to all species that every animal must protect its body and life, avoid those things that are about to do it harm, and seek carefully and provide for all things that are necessary for living, such as nourishment, shelter, and other associated requirements. Similarly common among all animals is the seeking of its kind for the purpose of procreation, and the care of that offspring that has been consequently generated. But between a man and a beast there is a great difference: the beast is moved by sense, but accommodates itself only to what is present, distinguishing little between the present and the past. Man, however, because he partakes in reason, and through this discerns consequences, sees the causes behind things, and is not ignorant of progress and antecedents. He compares similar things and connects present events as well as future events, easily seeing the path of survival laid out, and he can prepare to devote energy on these necessities.

[12] In the same way, Nature reconciles man to discourse and social life by the power of reason, and generates in man an exceptional love for those produced as his offspring. Nature also impels him to want to be part of assemblies and meetings with others. Further, it demands that he prepare those things that supply comforts and the needs of life, not only for himself alone, but also for his mate and children, whose protection ought to be his first concern. Nature kindles the spirit of man for these cares, and enlarges it for the completion of the effort.

---

[19] I.e., Panaetius.

38

[13] The search for and examination of truth is without doubt a special characteristic of man. So when we are free from the necessary cares and preoccupations of life, we find it pleasant to see, hear, and learn; we pursue the understanding of things hidden or wondrous for a fulfilling life. From this it may be discerned that what is true, simple, and sincere is most appropriate for the nature of man. To this zeal for seeking the truth, there is joined an appetite for a certain type of control, so that no one wants to submit to a soul well-informed by Nature except one instructed, taught, or governed according to principles of the common good and legitimacy. From this inclination arises greatness of soul, as well as a contempt for the mundane affairs of mankind.

[14] And it is no small thing that, due to the power of Nature and reason, man is the one animal that senses the meaning of order, of what ought to be done, with regard to both deeds and words. No other animal has such a deep sense for symmetry, beauty, and harmony. Similarly, Nature and reason, moving from the material world to the spiritual world,[20] may take care to preserve beauty, harmony, and order in discussion and deeds, so that nothing may be done indecorously or effeminately. And in thoughts and actions, they may take care that nothing is done wantonly.

From all these factors, we may forge and hammer out what we have thus far investigated, which is this: moral rectitude, although it may not be considered of noble origin, nevertheless still is supremely honorable. And what we can truly say is that although it is praised by none, it is still praiseworthy by its very nature.

V. [15] Marcus, my son, you indeed see here the same image, which is the face of moral rectitude. As Plato says, "If it is seen by mortal eyes, it arouses a passionate love of wisdom." All moral

---

[20] The phrase here is *ab oculis ad animum*, literally meaning "from the eyes to the soul."

goodness originates from four sources: (1) it is developed in the skilled examination of the truth; (2) in the protecting and developing of the society of man, with faithful observance for the rights of each man and his counterpart; (3) in a lofty and invincible spirit, possessing greatness and power; or (4) by the order and method in all things which happen and are debated, in which modesty and temperance are involved.

Although these four are intertwined and connected, nevertheless certain types of duties arise from each of these sources. Thus from that category which has been listed first in the order above (in which we place wisdom and prudence), we find investigation and the discovery of the truth. This is the special feature characteristic of that virtue.

[16] Whoever has examined these things closely to see what may be nearest to the truth, and who is able to see most acutely and perceptively, and to explain the underlying reasons for things: that person is considered to be the most prudent and wise. Truth is the sort of material with which this virtue deals, and what it is intimately associated with.

[17] To the three remaining virtues, however, are assigned the requirements related to those things needed for protecting and preserving of the action of life, so that the society and fellowship of men are served, and so that excellence and generosity of soul may be displayed, not only in increasing resources and advantages and providing for one's self and family, but much more in expressing disdain for these things. However, order, constancy and moderation, as well as qualities related to these things, inhabit the kind of lifestyle where a certain amount of action, and not just mental exercise, is needed. By the use of these things which are drawn out of life, and by employing a certain type of order and rhythm, we will preserve dignity and moral goodness.

VI. [18] Now out of the four subsets in which we have divided the nature and power of moral goodness, the first, which consists in the acquisition of knowledge, profoundly touches human nature. Indeed, we are all drawn and led by the craving for truth and knowledge. We think it beautiful to excel in the pursuit of these things. We consider it bad and disgraceful to slip, to err, to not know something, or to be deceived. In this matter, according to Nature and morality, two vices must be avoided. One is that we should not consider the unknown as known, and assent blindly to it. He who wishes to avoid this vice (and everyone should want to avoid it) will devote time and attention to careful consideration of this issue.

[19] The other vice is that some exert too great an effort and too much study on obscure and difficult things that are usually pointless. If these vices can be substituted with the expenditure of work and care on things morally good and worth thinking about, a man will be justly rewarded. We have heard of such a man, Caius Sulpicius, in the field of astrology; we also know of such a man in geometry named Sextus Pompeius.[21] There are many such men in the field of dialectics, and more in civil law. All of these arts are concerned with the investigation of truth; and yet to be diverted by such study away from the practical doings of life is against the idea of duty. The merit of all virtue consists in action.

A pause in this action may happen often; and many are given a chance to return to study. The activity of the mind, which never rests, is able to sustain us in the pursuit of knowledge, even without our scholarly work. However, all thought and activity of the mind will be focused either on deliberating on moral issues and those things pertaining to goodness and living well, or on the pursuits of knowledge and scholarship.

---

[21] Caius Sulpicius Gallus was a statesman, general, and astronomer. He was a man of wide learning. As a general, he predicted a lunar eclipse the day before the Battle of Pydna in 168 B.C. After his retirement from military affairs he devoted himself to astronomy. Sextus Pompeius (67--35 B.C.) was the youngest son of Pompey the Great and a general during the late republic. He was executed by Mark Antony.

Thus we have described the first source of duty.

VII. [20] Of the three remaining sources, the most expansive is known as that law by which the life of a society and a quasi-community is secured. There are two parts to this: *justice*, the most compelling of virtues, which is the criterion for judging men "good"; and linked to this, *kindness*, which one may also call benevolence or charity. But the first function of justice is to enforce the principles that (1) a man may harm no one except first provoked by injury; and (2) that common property should be used for the community and private property should be used individually.

[21] There is no such thing as private property in the state of nature. It comes about through occupation for a long period of time (as when someone takes possession of empty land), by annexation (as in the case of acquisition through war), or by law, treaty, contract, or chance. On this basis, the land of Arpinum is held by the Arpinates, and the Tusculan land by the Tusculans. A similar description applies to the possession of private property. From this principle, since the property of a man may once by nature have been part of community property, a man may hold what he has thereby obtained. And if another man so desires a private holding for himself, he will violate a basic law of human society.

[22] However, as Plato has eloquently written, we are not born and raised for ourselves alone: our country claims a part of us, as do our friends. And as the Stoics maintain that whatever comes from the earth is created for the use of all men, so men have been created for the sake of other men, so that they may be able to be of mutual benefit to each other. In this matter we ought to follow the lead of Nature, to bring common advantage in ordinary things by an exchange of duties, by giving and receiving, by good works, and by deploying knowledge. By such means men are bound together with other men in society.

[23] The beginning of all this is faith in justice. It is

steadfastness and truth in words and agreements. From this, although it may be seen by someone perhaps as rather awkward, nevertheless we may dare to imitate the Stoics, who studiously inquire into such things as where words have come from. We may believe that "faith" is so called because what is said to happen, actually comes about. There are two types of injustice. One type arises from those who cause it; the other type arises from those who are able to act, but do nothing to ward off injustices from happening to others. He who commits an assault on another, through anger or incited by some other disturbance, is seen almost as to lay a hand on a companion; and he who does nothing to defend against or prevent injury, if he can, behaves sinfully, as if he were deserting his parents, family, or friends.

[24] And often those injuries which are inflicted with deliberate harm in mind really proceed from fear; as he who thinks about harming another man worries that, if he does not do it, he himself may suffer some harm. They undertake the doing of injury, for the most part, to obtain that which they covet most. And this is why avarice remains the most pervasive type of vice.

VIII. [25] The riches of life are sought, however, for necessary things, and also for the enjoyment of pleasure. In those who have a greater spirit for such things, we see the love of wealth deployed with an eye to augmenting resources and increasing power. Marcus Crassus recently mused that a man did not have enough money to be ruler of a state unless he had sufficient personal funds to sustain his own army.[22] The trappings of pomp and the refinements of life in elegance and abundance are alluring, with the result that lust for money extends to infinity. The accumulation of personal property should not itself be

---

[22] Marcus Licinius Crassus (115—53 B.C.) is considered one of the richest men in Roman history. He perished in a disastrous campaign against the Parthian Empire in the east. He could afford to finance his own army.

condemned, provided it is harming no one. But failing to avoid such hoarding generally leads to trouble.

[26] A good many people, however, may be led greatly astray such that forgetfulness blinds them to justice when ambition for power or honors takes hold of them. As the poet Ennius says:

Neither sacred fellowship nor faith are principles of the throne.[23]

And this maxim is widely applicable. Whenever a situation arises in which it is not possible for many to be preeminent, competition among men rises to such a point where it becomes most difficult to preserve the idea of "sacred fellowship." The rashness of Julius Caesar, who perverted all human and divine law because he had become fixated on supreme power through wrong-headed thinking, showed itself in this way. On this topic, it is troublesome that among the souls of the greatest, most splendid, and most creative, we find a good many lovers of honor, power, command, and glory. This must be scrupulously avoided, lest an offense of this type be committed.

[27] But in every injustice there is a great difference, for each disturbance of the mind, between those that come about briefly and spontaneously, and those wrongs that arise from methodical planning and maneuver. Less serious, therefore, are those which come about by sudden unanticipated action, than are those which are the products of premeditation and preparation.

Enough has been said here regarding the infliction of injury.

IX. [28] There are often many reasons given in justifying the deserting of one's duty. People do not wish to take on the expense or labor, or incur the wrath of others; and through negligence, laziness, or inertia, such people may be impeded by preoccupation

---

[23] That is, as far as kings are concerned, there is little in the way of common cause. A king will do anything, regardless of moral principles.

with their own personal issues, so that they allow to be abandoned those whom they should protect. Thus it may be seen that what Plato said regarding philosophers might not be adequate, specifically when he said that philosophers were men of justice simply because they delved into the investigation of truth, and condemned and regarded as nothing the material things that most people sought out and squabbled over. They indeed bring about one type of justice, in that they inflict no active harm on anyone. But they help cause another type of harm, in that they desert those whom they ought to help, as a consequence of being hamstrung by their focus on bookish scholarship. Therefore, he believes such men should not take on the responsibility of public office except when they are compelled to do so. It would be better still if this came about voluntarily. For if something is right, it is just only insofar as it is voluntary.

[29] There are also those who, either from being absorbed in their own personal affairs or due to aversion to people in general, say that they are only taking care of their own business and see themselves as not harming anyone. Those who avoid one type of injustice fall into another: they abandon the society of life, because they share none of their labor, works, or abilities. Therefore, having laid out the two types of injustice and stating the appropriate causes of each type, and having described the rules by which justice is maintained, we can easily judge on every occasion what the right duty may be, unless we are very narcissistic.

[30] Certainly it is difficult to care for the affairs of others; and yet the playwright Terence has one of his characters, Chremes, think that "nothing human is alien to him."[24] Still, because we perceive and sense more acutely those things that bring us prosperity or adversity than those things which happen to

---

[24] *The Self-Tormentor* (in Greek, *Heauton Timorumenos*), 77.

other people, and which we see taking place from a long distance, we tend to judge things one way for ourselves, and one way for others. On account of this, when people are unsure if something is a good or bad action, they act wisely in hesitating to do anything at all. Justice reveals itself by its own light; doubt indicates the awareness of injustice.

X. [31] But there are times when those things that may seem appropriate for a just man, or whom we might call a good man, change and become something very different. To reciprocate an obligation, to honor a promise, and to become involved in other things related to truth and trust: matters such as these sometimes change, and may no longer serve the cause of justice. In such situations, we ought to refer back to that which was proposed as a first principle and the very foundation of justice: *first*, that no man should be harmed; and *finally*, that the common good be served. As things change with the times, moral duty correspondingly changes, and it may not be what it was originally.

[32] For it is possible that some promise may turn out badly for the person to whom it was made, or for the man who made the original promise. If, as the story goes, Neptune had not done what he had promised to Theseus, Theseus would not have been deprived of his son Hippolytus. As the story goes, of the three choices, this was the third: in a blind rage, he chose the death of his own Hippolytus.[25] And when this actually came to pass, Theseus was drowned in overwhelming grief. Therefore, no promises ought to be honored which are harmful to those whom you have made the promise; likewise, if they hurt *you* more than those for whom the promises were intended. It is not against moral duty to place the greater good before the lesser good.

Suppose, for example, you are about to go to court for a client

---

[25] See Euripides, *Hippolytus* 1315. In the myth, Hippolytus was killed as a consequence of his rejecting the advances of his stepmother Phaedra. She falsely accused Hippolytus of rape, and the enraged Theseus asked the god Neptune to punish the young man with death.

you have agreed to represent, and suddenly your son becomes gravely ill. It would not be a violation of your duty if you failed to do what you said you would do. The bigger issue would be that the person to whom you made the promise has himself no idea of the meaning of moral duty, if he complained of being abandoned. Who does not see that those promises should not stand, if someone is coerced by fear, or if a man makes a promise when deceived by guile? Indeed many of these cases are absolved by the ruling of a praetor, and sometimes by the legal codes.[26]

[33] Injustices often happen by a certain type of sophistry and an excessive deviousness, or by malicious interpretation of the law. It is from this situation that we have the well-worn proverb in general usage, "the more law, the more injustice." Many sins of this type are committed by states. This was the case when a military leader, having made a truce with the enemy for thirty days, still ravaged his fields by night, since (he claimed) the truce applied during "days" rather than nights. In this regard, we cannot even approve of the action of one of our own, if it is true what is said of Quintus Fabius Labeo (I have nothing but hearsay to support the following story).[27]

In arbitrating a dispute between Nola and Naples regarding their boundary decreed by the senate, he arrived at the location, met with each of them separately, and implored them to act without greed, and without petty grasping. He also asked them to make forward progress in discussions, rather than slide backwards. When each party did as he requested, there were some open fields left between the two parties. He then set the boundary to which the two parties had agreed; the parcel of land left over in

---

[26] Cicero capably argues here that coercion, duress, or exigent circumstances should mitigate a breach of contract. The praetor was an elected magistrate. They announced their legal rulings in case law that was known as *ius praetorium*. There were two praetors, just below consul in rank.

[27] He was consul in 183 B.C.

the middle he confiscated in the name of the Roman people. This is deception, not adjudication. Such deviousness is to be avoided in all things.

XI. Certain duties must be honored even to those from whom you have suffered injury. It is a matter that falls under the category of avenging and punishing. I do not know for certain if it is enough that he who provoked an injury should repent of his injustice, so that he and others might be slower to do such injury in the future.

[34] In the matter of nations, the laws of war must be scrupulously observed. There are two methods of disputing: one by discussion, and the other by force. The former is suited to man, and the latter is for wild beasts. We should take recourse in force only if we are unable to use the option of discussion. [35] Thus wars should only be undertaken for this reason: that a state may live in peace without external injury. And once the victory has occurred, we must spare those who have not been cruel or barbarous during the fighting. So our ancestors accepted as citizens the Tusculans, Aequians, Volscians, Sabines, and Hernicians, but destroyed utterly Carthage and Numantia.[28] I would not have wanted this for Corinth, but I believe there was some motivation; perhaps its location made its destruction a military necessity.[29]

Indeed, it is my opinion that peace is always desirable, provided it is one which has not come about by treacheries. In

---

[28] Numantia was a Celtiberian city-state destroyed by order of the senate in 153 B.C. Scipio Aemilianus Africanus commanded the operation. The Italic "nations" mentioned here were incorporated into the expanding Roman state. Tusculum was incorporated into Rome in 381 B.C., the Sabines and Volsicans in 286 B.C., the Hernicans in 306 B.C., and the Aequi in 302 B.C. Carthage, of course, was destroyed completely.

[29] Corinth was destroyed in 146 B.C. when Roman forces, commanded by Lucius Mummius, defeated the Achaean League. The city was stripped of its art treasures, which were then shipped to Rome.

fact, if I had been consulted on the matter, we might still have had some sort of republic, if even an imperfect one, whereas now we have none at all.

When those whom you have conquered by force lay down their arms and submit to our generals in good faith, even though the battering ram has smashed their walls, it is advisable to receive them civilly. This type of justice has, to a high degree, been cultivated by us. Those who offer guarantees of good faith to nations and states defeated in war become the patrons of those states, by the custom of our ancestors.

[36] The law of war was written in the most consecrated way under the fetial code of the Roman people.[30] And from this it is possible to understand that no war is just unless it is waged after formal demands have first been made, or after advance notice and a declaration. The general Popilius was in charge of a province, and in his army was serving the son of Cato as a recruit.[31] When Popilius was seen to dismiss one of the legions, Cato's son, who was serving in that legion, was also dismissed. But when the son remained in the army out of love for combat, Cato wrote to Popilius to say that if he allowed the son to stay in the new army, Popilius was obliged to administer a second military oath to the son, since by previously dismissing him, the son was unable by law to fight with the enemy.

[37] So here I point out the highest observance of the rules of conduct in waging war. Marcus Cato the Elder wrote a letter to

------

[30] The fetial code takes its name from a type of priest in ancient Rome. A fetial priest was one who advised the senate on treaties and on declarations of war. They were grouped into a *collegia* of twenty, and took the god Jupiter as their patron. Their general purpose seems to have been to ensure that Rome retained the protection of the gods in its relations with foreign states. *See* Livy, I.24 and I.32.

[31] Marcus Popilius Laenas (also spelled Popillius) was consul in 173 B.C. and was sent to subdue the Ligurians in northern Italy.

his son Marcus, stating that he had heard that his son had been dismissed by the consul while the son was a soldier in the war against Perseus in Macedonia. He therefore warned the son not to engage in battle: Cato the Elder claimed that it was not lawful for a soldier to engage in combat once he had been demobilized.

XII. I also notice that he who might be properly named an "enemy combatant" is called an "outsider," thus lightening the bitterness of the situation by a softer euphemism. The Latin word *hostis* ("enemy") was used by our ancestors to mean what we now call a "foreigner." The Twelve Tables show the same thing: "on a day set with a foreigner"; and "permanent authority granted in actions against a foreigner."[32] What can exceed such clemency, when you designate him with whom you are waging war with such mild words? Yet long usage has made this word (*hostis*) more harsh. It lost its significance as indicating a regular foreigner, and what remains is the idea of a person bearing arms.

[38] When there is a fight for power, and glory is sought through war, the same causes ought to underlie such contests, which I have stated above as the valid reasons for waging war. But these wars which are undertaken by the state for the sake of glory must be waged less harshly. Thus we deal with a citizen in one way if he is an enemy and another way if he is a competitor (since with the rival it is a matter of honor and dignity and with the enemy is a matter of life and reputation). War was waged with the Celtiberians and Cimbrians as if they were real enemies, not for influence, but for survival; whereas we fought with the Latins, Sabines, Samnites, Carthaginians, and with Pyrrhus of Epirus for political power. The Carthaginians were treacherous; Hannibal was cold-hearted; but the others were more equitable. King Pyrrhus, when returning prisoners, famously said this:

I ask not for gold, nor that you give me moneyed reward;

---

[32] The Law of the Twelve Tables (*Leges duodecim tabularum*) were the ancient foundation of Roman law, adopted around 449 B.C. *See* Livy III.57.10.

Not as play-actors in war, but as fighting belligerents
Let us stake our lives on the sword,
Not on gold, and see what may happen.
Whether Mistress Fortune decides for you or for me,
And whatever She may bring,
We put ourselves to the test with bravery.
And so hear this judgment:
Fortune showed consideration for those displaying bravery in war;
Certainly I grant these same men their liberty.
I give and grant them to you; let them go in peace
With the grace of the gods.[33]

Without doubt this is a truly regal conception, and one worthy of the house of Aeacidae.[34]

XIII. [39] If a situation arises when a man has made a promise to the enemy, he should honor such a promise also. During the First Punic War, Regulus was captured by the Carthaginians; his captivity was commuted and he was sent to Rome and ordered to return after conducting prisoner-exchange negotiations.[35] When he addressed the Senate, he recommended that Carthage's prisoners should not be returned to the enemy. Finally, when his family and friends tried to prevent him from returning to Carthage, he preferred to return there to face execution rather than to breach a promise given to the enemy.

[40] During the Second Punic War, after the Battle of Cannae, Hannibal sent ten prisoners to Rome under an oath that they should return to him unless they succeeded in releasing his own men who had been captured earlier. As long as any of them lived,

---

[33] Ennius, *Ann.* VI.

[34] A euphemism for Pyrrhus as King of Epirus. The kings of Epirus claimed descent from the mythical Aeacus, a supposed king of the island of Aegina in the Saronic Gulf.

[35] Marcus Atilius Regulus (c.307—250 B.C.) was a Roman statesman and general, and consul in 267 and 256 B.C.

the censors held them culpable and kept them in poverty, since technically they had committed perjury in breaking their oath to Hannibal.

When a man left Hannibal's camp with his permission, he returned a little later, saying that he had forgotten something (I have no idea what it was); and when he left the camp the second time, he thought his earlier oath to Hannibal no longer applied. In his mind, the semantics mattered more than the purpose behind the words. So, in matters of trust, always be cognizant of the purpose behind the words, not just the words themselves.

We have another great example from our ancestors regarding justice to an enemy. When a deserter from Pyrrhus's camp came to the senate and said that he would poison the king and cause his death, the senate and Caius Fabricius handed the deserter over to Pyrrhus.[36] Thus Fabricius refused even to approve of a scheme to murder by treachery an enemy who was at once powerful and waging active warfare against Fabricius's own country.

[41] Enough has been said regarding the moral duties of armed conflicts. We should remember, however, that justice must be served with regard to those who are most helpless. The lowest lot, and poorest fortune, is that of slaves. Those men speak rightly who counsel that slaves should be treated as hired workers: require them to work, but give them what they are owed. Injury may come about in either of two ways: by force or by fraud. Fraud belongs to the fox, and force to the lion; and both are contrary to the nature of a good man. Fraud, however, is more odious. Of all the types of injustice, none is more deadly than that perpetrated by those who profoundly deceive, while appearing to be good men. We have said enough here of justice.

XIV. [42] Finally, as was proposed above, we should say a

---

[36] Caius Fabricius Luscinus was consul in 282 and 278 B.C.

few words about kindness and courtesy.[37] Nothing is more agreeable to the nature of man than these qualities, but there are many potential pitfalls. First, it must be taken care that the courtesy[38] does not hurt the person granting it; that it not hurt the person to whom it is extended; and finally, that the courtesy not exceed the resources of the grantor. Of course, courtesy must be granted proportionately, on the principle of relative merit. This indeed is fundamental to the idea of justice, to which all things relate back. When a man bestows something on someone whom he intended to help, but which is actually harmful to him, the giver is neither a beneficent nor a generous man. He must be judged to be a pernicious yes-man. Further, those who harm some people so that they may be generous to others commit injustices in the same way, just as if they had converted others' property for their own personal use.

[43] Indeed, there are many lovers of glory and splendor who take from some people so that they may give to others; they believe they should be seen as generous to their friends, if they enrich them by any way possible. However, it is the furthest thing from proper duty, and nothing could be more contrary to the very idea of duty. Therefore we must take care, when using this sort of liberality, that if we help our friends, we do not harm anyone else. The transfer of large sums of money by Lucius Sulla and Caius Caesar from its lawful owners to others should not thus be seen as generosity. Nothing is honorable if it is not also just.

[44] Another point of caution is that generosity should not exceed one's resources. Those who want to be more beneficent than they can afford, commit in the first place the mistake of hurting their familial relations; those resources that might be

---

[37] The two words used here are *beneficentia* (beneficence, kindness) and *liberalitas* (courtesy, kindness).

[38] The word *benignitas* here is used, meaning kindness, courtesy, benevolence, or liberality.

transferred or left to heirs, are instead gifted to others. There exists in such liberality a love of plundering and liquidating one's assets in a self-defeating way, in order to create the resources needed for such largesse. One may see many people who are not by nature generous, but rather are glory-seekers. They do many things that arise more from a desire to chase after ostentation, than from an honest sense of good-will. Such a pretense is more connected to vanity than it is to either kindness or honesty.

[45] The third point is that, in matters of beneficence, the issue of worth must be considered. In deciding whether to confer a benefit on a man, his character must be looked at. We must first weigh his disposition towards us, and his record in society and the community, as well as his utility towards our own interests. It is optimal if all these factors come together; if they do not, then the more numerous factors, and the more important ones, are to be accorded the greater weight.

XV. [46] Because the men we live with are neither perfect men nor supremely wise, but conduct themselves well enough if they have in them a decent approximation of virtue, I believe it worth noting that no one should be neglected who displays some amount of virtue in him. However, a man who possesses to a great extent these kinder virtues—modesty, temperance, and justice, about which much here has been said—ought to be cultivated favorably. These virtues commonly are seen to be associated with a good man. A strong and great spirit in a man who is neither advanced in these virtues nor very wise is, for the most part, too unwieldy. Those virtues previously mentioned (i.e., modesty, temperance and justice) are what set apart a truly good man. So much for our discussion on these aspects of generosity.

[47] With regard to the person who may have goodwill towards us, the first moral duty is that we provide most for the man who esteems us the most. But this emotion is not like the ardent love of adolescents bordering on passion; we should judge it rather more like stability and constancy. But if there are already

rewards due to someone, such that thanks should be important but need not be mandatory, then greater care must be employed: for no duty is more important than giving thanks.

[48] The poet Hesiod tells us to give back in greater measure, if we are able, those favors which we accept for our use.[39] What should we then do when confronted by the receipt of an unexpected benefit? Should we imitate the fertile fields, which produce more than they receive? Indeed, if we do not hesitate to confer benefits on those whom we hope will be of future use to us, how should we behave to those who are providing us benefits now? Now there are two kinds of kindness: one, the giving of a benefit; and two, the returning of a benefit. Whether we give or not give is within our power. A good man should always return a kindness, as long as he is able to do it without injury.

[49] There should be some favorite out of the accepted benefits, so that without doubt the greatest return goes to him who gave the most. Nevertheless, it must be considered especially in what spirit and enthusiasm the kindness was made. Many people rashly do such favors for others, without judgment, prompted by a general malaise or rashness, their spirits animated as if by a sudden wind. These types of benefits must not be equated with those which are considerately and deliberately conferred with judgment. But in delivering a benefit and returning thanks, if everything else is equal, the best rule is that aid should be granted to him who needs help the most. Many people do the opposite: they become most submissive to the person from whom they expect to get the most, even if this person has no need of them.

XVI. [50] The society of man, and its common fellowship, will best be aided if kindness is normally conferred on those to whom we are most connected. But with regard to the principles of Nature that belong to human society and community, it is clear

---

[39]*Works and Days*, 349-351.

that they are of very old lineage. The first principle is what is found in every type of human society: this is the bond of reason and speech. By teaching, learning, communicating, debating, and judging, it brings men together and joins them in a type of natural association. In nothing else are we further removed from the nature of animals. For we often say that they possess courage, such as that found in horses and lions; but we do not say that they have a sense of justice, equity, or benevolence, for they are lacking in reason and speech.

[51] So this is the most common accessible bond existing among men, and among all in society. The community must preserve all things that Nature produces for the common use of men. As is laid out in the legal codes and the civil law, some things are owned as those laws so decree. For other things, it can be said that "friends own everything as a community," as goes the old saying of the Greeks.[40] The community property of all men can be found in the types of things described by the poet Ennius; he proposed it in one instance, but it can be reworked to more universal applicability:

A man, who graciously shows the way to a wayward traveler,
Almost creates a light ignited by the lamp of another man.
It gives off no less light than his, when he will have thus lit it for him.

From this, the poet teaches that we ought to bestow on a stranger those necessities that we can provide without harming our own interests.

[52] From this idea we have the following generalized sayings: "Don't deny someone the water that flows by"; "Tolerate the taking of some fire from your own fire"; "If a man wants it, give him advice if he is pondering the right course." These actions

---

[40] See Plato, *Phaedrus* 279 C.

have utility to those in need, and the giving does not harm the giver. Thus we should always strive to do such things, and contribute something for the common use. But because the resources of individuals are limited, and the quantity of those in need is infinite, the generosity of the common man must fall back on the principle of Ennius, stated above: "It gives off no less light than his." For we must still preserve the ability to be generous with our own kinsmen.

XVII. [53] However, there are many positions of men in society. As we move away from this universal principle, we find a more intimate one, in which men are joined closely by race, nation and language. Closer still is the bond joining men in the same "polis."[41] Fellow citizens in such a state share many things in common: a forum, temples, porticos, roads, laws, legal systems, courts and voting rights. We also find customs, intimacies and formalized business arrangements binding all such citizens together. But there is a closer bond among close familial relations in society. From the immensity of the population of the entire human race, this principle is thus circumscribed within a small and confining boundary.

[54] So that they preserve the will to procreate, this nature is the common possession of all animals: the first partnership is that of marriage, the second is the bond to one's children, and finally comes the domicile, with its shared common living. This is the founding principle of any city-state, and acts as a sort of incubator of a republic. Following after this are the bonds between brothers and sisters, and from there the bonds between first cousins and then second cousins. When they are not able to be kept in one household, extended family members go out to reside in other places, as if they were colonists. Then come marriages and those related by marriage, and from these yet more close relations; the origin of republics is found in the propagation and dissemination

---

[41] The word used here is *civitas*, meaning commonwealth or city-state.

of these tendrils of kinship. Bonds of blood tie men together through benevolence and affection; it is a great thing to have the same shrines to one's ancestors, as well as to have religious rites and tombs in common.

[55] Yet of all social bonds, none is more excellent, and more enduring, than when good men of similar ways are joined together in a spirit of familiarity. This masculine goodness (about which we often speak), if we discern it in another, draws us to him and makes us friends with him who has this quality.

[56] Although all virtue draws us to it and molds us, so that we hold in high esteem those who are seen to possess it, justice and generosity do this to the greatest extent. Nothing is more pleasant and intimate than the resemblance of men of good character, in which the same spirit and the same purpose can be found, so that each may equally be a source of delight to the other. From this may be produced what Pythagoras wanted in friendship: the idea that one "being" may be fused out of several. Another great type of fellowship is one which is formed by the giving and receiving of mutual benefits. When such benefits are mutual and agreeable, those with whom they are established are bound together in a robust society.

[57] Yet when we review things with the greatest reason and personal feeling, it is clear that in all societies, there is no social bond more important, or more dear, than that which binds each man to his own country. Parents, children, relatives and family members are all dear to us; but of these, only "country" embraces all of these categories. What good man would hesitate to meet death, if he might be able to offer his native land a vital service? The barbarity of those who torment their country with every sort of crime--who are and have been obsessed with completely destroying it--is thus even more detestable.[42]

---

[42] This sentence appears to be a reference to Cicero's anti-republican political enemies, namely Caesar, Antony, and Catiline.

[58] But if an argument and comparison were to be made regarding to whom the moral obligations of most men should be given, the primary recipients would be parents and country. It is to them that we are bound by the greatest responsibilities. After this come children and the members of our household, who see us as their sole means of support. Finally come our other relatives, with whom each of us has a common fortune. For this reason, the necessary protections of life are most owed to those of whom I spoke earlier. However, common life interests and nourishment, advice, conversations, encouragements, consolations, and sometimes disapproval thrive best in friendships. The most perfect friendship is that which unites likeness of personal characteristics.

XVIII. [59] In the assignment of all these duties, we must consider what is most necessary for each individual person, and what each person can accomplish with or without our help. Thus the degrees of necessity are not the same as the types of situations. There are duties which ought to be more important to some than to others. For example, you would sooner help a neighbor in gathering his crops than a brother or a friend; but if there were a case in court, you would rather defend a family member or a friend, than a neighbor. These things, therefore, must be surveyed in every situation involving duty (as well as in every custom and practice), so that we can be good evaluators of moral duties in general, and to see by adding and deducting various factors what the chief remaining point may be, from which we will know what duty is properly owed to whom.

[60] As neither doctors, military commanders, nor orators can arrive at great achievements in their professions without diligence and experience—even if they know the rules of their trades—so the principles underlying the rules of moral duties are formed in the same way as we are now describing them. The magnitude of the task demands work and practical experience. We have now said enough regarding these things that exist in the laws of human

society (to the extent that moral goodness is concerned), from where the idea of duty first originates.

[61] It must be understood that moral goodness and moral duty come from the four types of virtue that have been proposed. If we can implement these concepts, it would be a most splendid thing, because we are thereby engaging a great and lofty spirit, one that is contemptuous of petty worldly affairs. Thus it would be a great insult if someone were to say:

> You, young men, display the soul of a woman,
> While this girl here displays that of a man,

and with this same idea:

> Salmacidan, get spoils without blood or sweat.[43]

From the opposite perspective, in the matter of great achievements which are done bravely and excellently with a noble spirit, I suspect that we offer more fulsome praise. Thus there is never a shortage of orators to talk about Marathon, Salamis, Plataea, Thermopylae, and Leuctra, and even our own Cocles, the Decii, Gnaeus and Publius Scipio, Marcus Marcellus, and a great many others; and most importantly, of course, our own Roman people which excels in nobility of spirit.[44] Enthusiasm for glory derived from war is shown, of course, when we see statutes adorned in military decorations.

---

[43] The reference here is to a person who behaves like Salmacis. Salmacis in Greek mythology was a nymph or naiad who lived a life of wanton luxury. There was also a water fountain located near the Mausoleum of Halicarnassus with this name, which according to legend made effeminate all men who drank from it (*See* Strabo XIV.2.16).

[44] Horatius Cocles was a military hero of the old republic; his famous stand on a bridge halted an Etruscan attack in the late 6th century B.C. The Decii were a famous family who became renowned for the sacrifices made by their members in preserving Rome, especially Publius Decius, tribune in 120 B.C.

XIX. [62] This glorification of the human spirit, which is found in hardships and labors, is nothing but a vice if justice is absent, and it fights not for the good of the community but for individual gains. This is not only *not* virtue, but rather repellent savagery against all. Thus "fortitude" is rightly defined by the Stoics when they describe it as the virtue that fights for justice. For this reason, no one attains the glory of achievement by treachery and guile; nothing can be honorable when justice is absent.

[63] The following saying of Plato is most appropriate: "Not only must all knowledge disconnected from justice be called guile rather than wisdom; but also, a spirit prepared to confront danger, if driven by its own selfishness rather than the good of the community, should be called recklessness rather than true bravery."[45] Thus we want men to be strong and high-minded, and at the same time honest and guileless, friends of truth and not at all duplicitous. For these traits represent the common merit of justice.

[64] But this is problematic, because obstinacy and love of power readily come from this aggrandizement and potency of spirit mentioned above. As Plato tells us that the whole national character of the Lacedaemonians[46] was inflamed by the love of victory, so it is with anyone who excels in personal spirit. He mainly wants to be the first among his peers, or rather the sole leader. It is difficult, however, when one desires to be first among all others, to serve the cause of equity, which is the greatest characteristic of justice. The result of this is that such men do not tolerate the restraint of their behavior by public discussion, nor of any restraint set by public or legitimate law. In a republic they are,

---

[45] Cicero has done some splicing here. The first part of this quote is from the *Menexemus*, 246E. The second part is from *Laches* 197B.

[46] I.e., Spartans.

for the most part, found as bribers and seditious types, seeking the greatest spoils of power, and striving to be superior through force, rather than equal through justice. But what is more difficult, is what is more glorious; and there is no situation from which justice ought to be absent.

[65] Thus, the strong and brave must be considered not those who cause injury, but those who avert it. True and wise greatness of spirit, however, judges goodness (as Nature also does) by what deeds are actually done, rather than just by fame; and it prefers to be the first principle in reality, rather than in appearance. For he who depends on the fickleness of the ignorant multitude must not be considered a truly great man. The more deep-rooted a soul's love of glory may be, the more easily it is driven to unjust acts. This is indeed a slippery slope. For hardly a man may be found who, having undertaken great labors and placing himself in harm's way, will not then want glory as some sort of reward for his troubles.

XX. [66] A strong and great soul is altogether distinguished by two features. One is the contempt for the external things of this world. The great soul is persuaded that no man ought to wonder at, hope for, or seek after anything except those things related to goodness and virtue, and that he should succumb to neither another man, nor a disturbance of the spirit, nor a trial of Fortune. The second feature is that, when you have molded your soul with this sort of attitude, as I said above, you perform great achievements of the highest utility which are extremely arduous, laborious, and full of danger to life and to many other things related to one's livelihood.

[67] Of these two features of a great soul, all splendor and greatness (and I may also add utility) come from the latter quality, but the origin and reason for making men great derives from the former. In the former feature is that quality which makes souls great and contemptuous of baser things. This same thing is separated into two aspects: *first*, that you judge moral goodness to

be the only good; *second*, that you are free from all distress of the soul. We must remember that, with regard to those things seen by the majority as attractive and wonderful, there are a select few great souls who will look down on these same things as unworthy, and disdain them as firm and stable life principles. A robust soul, and great constancy, are also needed to bear the bitter experiences of life, which Fortune often and in unexpected ways visits on us, so that you are in no way deflected from your natural course, or from the dignity of human wisdom.

[68] It would not make sense for him who is not paralyzed by fear, to be then ruined by lust. And it is not better for him who is unconquered by exertions, to be then destroyed by pleasures. For this reason, we must avoid these things, and shun the love of money. Nothing quite so reveals a narrow and small soul as the love of riches, and there is nothing more honest and beautiful than not to obsess about money, if one does not have it; and if one have it, to put it to uses related to kindness and generosity. You must also beware of the love of glory, as I said above; it snatches away one's freedom, for which all great men ought to struggle. A man should never seek absolute power; rather, he should either not accept it, or on occasion set it aside voluntarily.

[69] One must be free from all disturbances of the spirit, whether it be excessive desire or fear, sorrow, pleasure, or anger, so that tranquility and peace of the soul come about. For these in turn bring constancy and dignity. There are and have been many men who, searching for this very thing which I am speaking of, have removed themselves from public affairs and taken refuge in leisure. Among these are counted the most noble philosophers and by far the best leaders, as well as certain serious and focused men, all unable any longer to bear the habits of the mob or its leaders; they lived on their country estates, content to manage their personal affairs. [70] They had the same goal as that held by kings: that they need nothing, that they answer to no one, and that they enjoy the benefit of true liberty, the distinguishing characteristic of which is to live as one wants.

XXI. This desire is held in common by lovers of power, of whom I have already spoken, and by men out of office as well. One group thinks it can get what it wants if it possesses great wealth, and the other group, if it only makes use of what little it has. These sentiments should not be entirely condemned for either group. The life of men of leisure is easier, safer, and less oppressive and troublesome to others; but the type of men who devote themselves to public life and to accomplishing great things is more productive and more suitable to achievement and greatness.

[71] Therefore, perhaps it should be allowed that some men, who by virtue of their intellectual abilities have devoted themselves to scholarship, may not take on the responsibility of public service. We must make a similar allowance for those men who, due to some physical ailment or affliction by some other serious condition, turn away from public affairs, as they concede the power and glory of leadership to others. For those other men who have none of these excuses, and say that they despise the civil and military offices that many are in fact in awe of, I believe this to be shameful, and much like a vice. With regard to those who think this way—who condemn glory and think it to be nothing— it is difficult not to concede that they may have a point. On the other hand, it seems that in reality they fear the hardships and anguish of political turbulence and its attendant strife, which they well know might bring them defeat and dishonor. There are also men who show little consistency in directly opposite situations. For example, they may denounce pleasures severely, and yet go soft in the face of physical pain; they may spurn glory, but go to pieces when disgraced. And even in these things, they may not act consistently!

[72] But for those other men, who possess the natural ability to accomplish great tasks, it is better that they set aside all hesitation, and seek public office and government service. In no other way may the state be governed or greatness of spirit be personally displayed. Those who hold the reins of state power, no

less than philosophers (I hardly know which type of man needs it more), must possess a certain nobility and that indifference to human affairs about which I often speak, as well as a tranquility and strength of spirit, so that they will be free from stress, and able to live with dignity and firmness.

[73] These difficulties are more easily borne by philosophers, who face in their lives less of those unwelcome gifts of Fortune, and require less of the special considerations noted above. Not only this, but if something unwelcome hits them, they fall less hard than the man in the public eye. Thus it is not without good reason that greater commotions of the soul are aroused by, and much more personal intensity is associated with, those who deal with matters of governance, when compared to those who have retired from public life. Such men have a more compelling need for spiritual fortitude and freedom from anxiety.

He who hopes to enter the waters of politics should try to consider these matters from the correct perspective. His intentions should be honest and he should have the requisite abilities; and he must also take care not to abandon rashly his ultimate goal through faintheartedness, or to become overconfident from a lust for power. Before going down any of these roads, then, a man ought to make diligent preparations.

XXII. [74] Many people consider the achievements of war to be greater than those of quiet contemplation. But this view is flawed. A good many men chase after war because of love for glory; this sentiment is connected with those possessing great spirits and strong characters. The sentiment is still greater for those who are talented in the military arts and fond of waging war. But if we wish to judge fairly, it must be said that many refinements of peace have proven to be greater and more noteworthy than the achievements of war.

[75] However much Themistocles is praised in book and song and his name ranked as more important than Solon's, and although Salamis has become the stuff of legend as the witness of his greatest victory (which causes his name to rank above that of

Solon, who set up the Areopagus), Solon's name must not be viewed as less important than the name of Themistocles.[47] The victory at Salamis was useful only once, but Solon's work was of enduring value to the state. By his guidance the laws of the Athenians and the foundations of civil order were permanently enshrined. Indeed, Themistocles could have spoken of no occasion where he himself helped the Areopagus. The Areopagus, on the other hand, truly helped him. His senate was an advisory body for waging war, and Solon had created this body himself.

[76] The same thing can be said regarding Pausanias and Lysander. Although the power of the Spartans is believed to have been acquired through the actions of these two men, their legacies must be accounted as minimal when compared with the laws and discipline of Lycurgus.[48] It was for these reasons in the first place that these two generals had powerful armies. For me, I do not believe when I was young that Marcus Scaurus should take the place of Caius Marius or, when I was involved in politics, that Quintus Catulus should take the place of Gnaeus Pompey.[49] Arms

---

[47] The ancient Areopagus in Athens was something like the Roman Senate. It functioned both as a council of elders and as a sort of high court. It was reformed in 594 B.C. by the great lawmaker Solon (Cicero somewhat imprecisely says that Solon "set it up" (quo primum constituit Areopagitas), when in fact Solon reformed what already existed). Themistocles (524-459 B.C.) was the Athenian general and statesman in command during the famous naval battle at Salamis (480 B.C.) during the second Persian invasion of Greece.

[48] Pausanias was an influential Spartan general of the fifth century B.C. Lysander was a Spartan general who presided over the Athenian defeat in the Peloponnesian War. Lycurgus was the legendary lawmaker of Sparta.

[49] Marcus Scaurus (163—89 B.C.) was a great politician of the republic and consul in 115 B.C.; Caius Marius (157—86 B.C.) was a general and statesman. There were two politicians of the name Quintus Lutatius Catulus. They were father (149—87 B.C.) and son (120—61 B.C.). The point here is to show that lawmakers are more important than generals.

are of little value abroad, unless there is prudent counsel at home.[50]

In the same way, Scipio Africanus, a great man and military commander, was not more useful to the republic in destroying Numantia, than at the same time was Publius Nasica in doing away with Tiberius Gracchus.[51] This of course is not purely a civil matter (it touches on warfare, as military force was implicated); but it was, nevertheless, accomplished through political action, without the use of the army.

[77] The following saying sums it up best. I hear it is in the habit of being used when a man is being attacked by those who are wicked and malevolent:

Arms make way for the toga, and laurels submit to praise.[52]

Even setting aside other examples, did not arms submit to the toga, when I was in a leadership position of the republic?[53] The danger to the republic was never more serious, nor the sense of leisure more extensive. Because of my counsels and attentiveness, weapons quickly slipped from the hands of the most desperate citizens and dropped to the ground. What comparable thing like

---

[50] This is a wonderful maxim, and is worth repeating in the original: *Parvi enim sunt foris arma, nisi est consilium domi.*

[51] Numantia was a Celtiberian city destroyed by Scipio the Younger (Africanus) in 133 B.C. Publius Nasica was a consul involved in the murder of the reformer Tiberius Gracchus, whom Cicero sees as a threat to the republic.

[52] Cicero uses "arms" here to symbolize force and violence, and "laurels" in the sense of the military honors bestowed on victorious generals. Such laurels are replaced ("submit") by praise given to civil administrators. So the point is to emphasize the preeminence of civil over military authority. This line is apparently from Cicero's lost epic poem *De temporibus suis* (*On His Times*), a description of political events of his era.

[53] This is a reference to Cicero's unmasking and defeat of the armed conspiracy of Catiline.

this was ever done in war? What general's bestowed triumph was so great?

[78] My son Marcus, if I may brag a little: the legacy of the glory and the facts of my deeds are there for your imitation. Gnaeus Pompeius, without doubt a great man praised for his achievements in war, honored me when he said within earshot of many others, that he would have achieved his third triumph in vain, had he not, through my services to the republic, been provided a place in which to conduct the triumph. But there are also civic examples of strength that are not inferior to military ones. In civil courage, indeed, considerably more efforts and devotions must be exerted.

XXIII. [79] As a whole, this strength of character which we seek with a surpassing, magnificent spirit is brought about by one's inner soul, not by the physical strength in a man's body. Nevertheless, the body must be exercised and hardened, so that it is able to obey the commands and guidance needed in pursuing great efforts and in tolerating labor. This moral character, which we seek in these pages, is placed completely in the care and inner workings of the soul. And certainly those men who wear the toga, and handle the work of guiding the republic, provide no less a useful service than those men who wage war. Often by their wise counsel wars are either not launched, or are concluded; and sometimes they are even advocated, as in the case of Marcus Cato in the Third Punic War.[54] His authority was paramount in that instance, even after his death.

[80] For this reason, seeking to adjudicate disputes through reason is better than deciding things by battlefield valor, but we must beware lest fleeing unconditionally from war becomes more important than the needs of justice. War should be undertaken in

---

[54] Marcus Cato (the Elder, 234–149 B.C.) was the famous advocate for the destruction of Carthage by constantly ending his speeches in the Senate with a rhetorical tag that the city must be destroyed.

a way that it clearly has peace as its sole object. One needs a strong and even-tempered spirit not to be thrown into confusion by bitter adversity, or rattled by being shaken from one's position, as we might say; rather, what is needed is presence of mind, so that one does not flee from the proper course, or from reason itself.

[81] Achieving this state of mind calls for a great intellect: being able to foresee how future events will play out and to visualize them; what can happen in all details and what things must be done beforehand; and when something happens, never being forced by circumstances to say, "I had not considered that." These are the workings of a great and surpassing soul, assured of its prudence and careful deliberation. However, to grapple with an enemy personally, and to fight hand-to-hand, is a savage and brutal affair. But when the situation or necessity calls for it, the fighting must be done on the ground by hand, so to speak, and death must be preferred to servitude or dishonor.

XXIV. [82] With regard to sacking and destroying cities, it must be very carefully considered that nothing be done rashly or cruelly. The responsibility falls on great men, when certain situations come about, to punish the guilty and to safeguard the innocent majority, so as to preserve the right balance of a good and positive Fortune. As I said above, just as there are many who have a higher regard for war than for the refinements of peace, you will also find many to whom reckless and hot-tempered advice seems more seductive and powerful than counsel based on careful, rational consideration.

[83] Fleeing from danger must never be done in a way to make us appear timid or irresolute; and we must also beware that we do not needlessly expose ourselves to harm. Nothing could be more foolish. For this reason we must imitate the practice of physicians in dealing with dangers: they treat mildly sick people with mild remedies, but are compelled to employ experimental and more dangerous treatments in cases of serious illness. For only a lunatic hopes for a storm when all is tranquil; a wise man will look for

rational ways to survive a storm. This is especially true when there is more to gain from an issue unfolding in a good way, rather than when a dubious issue might produce a bad outcome.

Those who undertake significant actions in public service subject partly themselves, and partly the state, to great dangers. In such matters, some forfeit their lives, and some forfeit the goodwill of their fellow citizens. We ought to be more willing to put ourselves at risk than the general community, and more ready to risk reputation and honor than other tangible assets.

[84] There have been found many men prepared to expend their lives for the sake of their country, and yet not want to make the same sacrifice for the sake of their ambition, even if the sacrifice were needed for the nation's sake. We see this in the case of Callicratidas, who had won many victories as a Spartan commander during the Peloponnesian War.[55] All his efforts ultimately ended in failure, as he was not willing to listen to the advice of those who thought he should remove his fleet from the Arginusae and not engage the Athenians in battle. His answer to them was that if the Spartans lost their fleet, they could build another, but he himself could not withdraw without the appearance of dishonor. And yet the damage he caused the Spartans was middling. More destructive was the action of Cleombrotus who, from fear of criticism, rashly engaged his enemy counterpart Epaminondas, and caused the power of the Spartans to be destroyed.[56]

---

[55] He was sent in 406 B.C. to replace Lysander and take charge of naval operations in the Aegean. He was considered a traditionalist, old-school Spartan.

[56] Cleombrotus I, a Spartan king of the Agiad line, was killed in action in the Battle of Leuctra 371 B.C. while engaging Epaminondas. The battle was a complete disaster for Sparta.

How much better were the fortunes of Quintus Maximus![57] About him the poet Ennius says:

One man saved our country by a policy of delay.
He never elevated his reputation over our safety,
And now after this, and so much greater, the glory of the man shines.[58]

This same type of mistake must also be avoided in politics. For there are those who, through fear of criticism, do not dare to say what they truly think, even though they may know it to be the best course of action.

XXV. [85] Thus all who propose to take charge of political affairs should adhere to the following two Platonic principles: *one*, that they should guard the interests of the citizens in such a way that in everything they do, they place their own interests second to those of the people; and *two*, that they care for the people as a whole, rather than favor the interests of one faction over the common good. This tutelage, this management of the affairs of a republic, must be carried out for the benefit of those whom such a guardian is tasked with protecting, and not for the benefit of the guardian himself. Those who look after the interests of one part of the population, and neglect the other parts, introduce a pernicious element in civil affairs: sedition and discord. And from this comes the situation where some favor the masses, and some favor the elites, and few favor the whole.

[86] For this reason the Athenians experienced great civil discord; and in our own republic we saw not only open sedition, but also pestilential civil wars. A serious and strong man, worthy

---

[57] Quintus Fabius Maximus Verrucosus Cunctator (280—203 B.C.), the Roman general who used a policy of delay and waiting to wear down Hannibal in the Second Punic War.
[58] *Ann.* XII.

of a leadership position in a state, will despise such a predicament, and do all he can to avoid it; and he will devote himself completely to his nation, grasping for neither riches nor his own aggrandizement. He will safeguard his country to the best of his ability, so that the interests of all are looked after. He will never call for baseless criminal charges to be filed against anyone out of spite or malice, and he will altogether adhere to the principles of justice and honesty. He will remain true to these principles, however much he is seriously hurt in upholding them, and will be prepared to face death rather than desert them, as I have noted above.

[87] Most unfortunate is the hunger and striving for honors.[59] Plato had a most lucid comment on this same matter when he said, "Those who dispute among themselves to see which one of them should guide the republic are similar to sailors who quarrel with each other to see which is most capable of steering a ship."[60] He also counsels us that "we should consider as enemies those who take up arms against the state, and not those who want to protect the republic according to their own judgment."[61] This was the nature of the dispute between Publius Africanus and Quintus Metellus, although it took place without ill-feeling between the two.

[88] And neither should we listen to those who believe in raging openly against one's opponents, and hold that this behavior is the mark of a great and strong man. Nothing is more commendable, nothing more worthy of a great and distinguished man, than clemency and a sense of benign forbearance. In a free

---

[59] By the word "honors" used here, Cicero means the *cursus honorum*, the sequence of public offices that aspiring politicians sought after as they hoped to reach the rank of consul. His intention is thus to condemn the obsessive quest for political office.

[60] See *Republic*, VI.488B and 489C.

[61] *Republic*, VIII.567C and *Laws*, IX.856B.

people, governed with equality before the law, levity and a certain loftiness of spirit must be cultivated, as I have previously discussed. This is necessary so that we do not continually grow angry at people approaching us for annoying matters, or asking us impudent questions. Otherwise, we will begin to become ineffective due to repressed rage and overt peevishness. Nevertheless mildness and clemency in human relations must be recommended for precisely the reason that, where matters of state are concerned, strictness must be adhered to, without which it is not possible to rule a country. All censures and reprimands should be free from insulting behavior, and such discipline should be meted out in a way that benefits the state, and not the person who does the punishing or the castigating.

[89] We must also beware that the punishment is not greater than the level of culpability for an offense; and that some may be indicted for a crime while others are barely called to account for the same transgression. It is absolutely forbidden that anger should be a factor in punishment. An angry man will never be able to hold a middle course in administering punishment, which should be somewhere between excessive and mild. This concept was endorsed by the Peripatetics, and rightly so, but only if we discount their praising of anger, and insistence that it is a gift of the gods. Anger should be repudiated in all situations. Those who guide the ship of state should be similar to the laws, which are guided not by anger, but by fairness.

XXVI. [90] When good things are happening abundantly in our lives, and all is going along as we like, let us avoid arrogance, haughtiness, and pride. Just as we bear adversity with calmness and levity, we must also enjoy prosperity with the same countenance, as we should in all parts of life, adhering to the same attitude of Socrates and Caius Laelius.[62] Philip, king of Macedon, who was exceeded by his son Alexander in deeds and glory, was still, I believe, superior to his son in good nature and humanity. Thus the former was always great, and the latter often quite shameful. Panaetius, the pupil and close friend of Africanus, says that he was accustomed to saying: "Just as horses, which have become difficult to manage because of their frequent participation in battles, are turned over to trainers so that they can be more easily handled, so too must men who have become arrogant and over-confident through repeated success be placed in the training-arena of reason and teaching, so that they may better appreciate the foolishness of human affairs, and the variability of Fortune."

[91] Furthermore, as a secondary matter, the counsel of friends must be relied on, and we should give such advice priority in authority. At the same time, we must beware lest we open our ears to flatterers, and permit ourselves to be fawned over. We will eventually come to see ourselves as worthy of flattery as a matter of right, and from this innumerable moral offenses spring up. Men so inflated by this sort of obsequiousness are ridiculed shamelessly by others, and are led to ruin by their errors. But let us move on from this subject.

[92] One other matter must still be judged. Those who direct public affairs, and whose administration extends the widest and affects the most people, bear the greatest burdens and possess the greatest spirits. There are and have been many men, after having left public office, who either pursue their own important studies or limit themselves to their own personal affairs. Some place themselves in a middle position between philosophers and men of public administration. They were satisfied with managing their own household matters, not trying to add to their holdings by any

---

[62] Caius Laelius was a prudent friend of Scipio Africanus and helped him in his Iberian campaign of 210-206 B.C.

possible way, nor excluding their kinsmen from the enjoyment of them, but rather sharing them with their worthy friends and with the state, if there were ever a need for this.

In the first place, such property should not be the rewards of disgraceful or morally odious effort. Secondly, it should be increased only by honesty, diligence and parsimony. Finally, it should be made available for the use of the worthy, and should adhere to the principles of beneficence and liberality, rather than to frivolity and indulgence. By keeping these principles in mind, one may be able truly to live nobly and eminently, and at the same time simply, faithfully, and as a friend to mankind.

XXVII. [93] Before moving on we must identify the one remaining component of moral goodness. In it we find a sense of modesty and, as it were, a certain garnishment to life. In this component is found temperance, modesty, and all calming of the soul's perturbations and other disorders. Under this heading is contained what may in Latin be called *decorum*. In Greek it is called *prepon*. Its power is such that it cannot be separated from moral goodness.

[94] What is right, is morally good; and what is morally good, is right. The nature of the difference between moral rectitude and decorum is easier to feel than to explain. Whatever "being right" may be, it is clear that honesty must come first. So not only in this part of moral goodness, which is to be discussed here, but also from the three preceding components, it is now apparent what "rightness" is. For to use reason and speech prudently, and to do what one does with deliberation, and to perceive what is true and to guard such truth: *this* is rightness. On the other hand, to be deceived, to follow the wrong path, to chase delusions, is as bad as being insane, and to have one's mind held hostage. All just things are right, and all unjust things bad, in the same way as is moral turpitude.

We see this same relationship when discussing fortitude. What is done in a manly way, and with a bold spirit, is worthy of a man and carries a certain distinction. What is done in violation of this spirit is contemptible, and exceedingly unworthy of a man.

[95] This decorum, I maintain, extends to all types of moral goodness, and it is so closely related to these that it does not require any recondite reasoning to perceive. A certain sense of decorum may be sensed in every virtuous act; but this can be separated from virtue more as a matter of theory than in reality. As beauty and shapeliness of the body cannot really be separated from the concept of health, so this decorum of which we speak is often confused with virtue, but still may be distinguished if we apply our minds and use careful thought.

[96] The classification of decorum is, however, two-fold. (1) We perceive a certain decorum in a general sense which permeates all types of moral goodness. (2) There is another type of decorum (subcategorized under the first type), which pertains individually to each category of moral goodness. The former is usually in the habit of being defined in this way: decorum is that which is in harmony with the excellence of man, as pertains to those things in which his nature differs from that of unreasoning animals. The other type of decorum (the subordinate type) is defined as that decorum which is in accord with Nature, such that it includes moderation and temperance, in the manner of a well-bred gentleman.

XXVIII. [97] For these things to be understood properly, we can take a closer look at the type of decorum that the poets aim for. More will be said on this matter in another place. Now the poets watch over decorum, we say, when the actions and statements of each individual person is worthy of their characters. Suppose that if Aeacus or Minos said:

Let them hate, while they may still fear,

Or:

The parent is the tomb of his own child,[63]

We would then see these statements as inappropriate, since we believe these characters to have been just. Yet when Atreus speaks these lines, they generate approval, since the statements are worthy of the character. It is for the poet to judge what is right for each character. Nature herself has stamped a persona on each of us with surpassing excellence and superiority over other living things.

[98] Thus, the poet will see to it that, out of the great variety of his characters, vice and good conduct are doled out in a way that accords with the characters. But for us, Nature has given us a measure of constancy, moderation, temperance and modesty. She also counsels us not to act in a way that may hurt our fellow man. It is in this way that we may see how decorum, which pertains in general to all moral goodness, may be spread widely; and we can also see how decorum shows itself in each category of virtue. For just as corporeal beauty, with all the right proportions of the limbs, excites the eyes and enchants us by its grace when all the parts interact with fluency, so this decorum, which illuminates a good life, arouses the approbation of those with whom it interacts by the order, constancy and moderation that are found in the words and actions of one who possesses it.

[99] A certain deference, therefore, must be shown with regard to all men: not just for the best ones, but for all the rest as well. For to be consciously unaware of what another man believes is not only arrogant, but also altogether negligent. There is a difference between justice and respect when one's relations to

---

[63] These lines are from the poet Lucius Accius (also called Lucius Attius), a Roman poet and scholar who lived from 170-86 B.C. His work is preserved only in fragments. The lines here are from his play, the *Atreus*. Aeacus was a legendary king of the island of Aegina in the Aegean Sea. Minos was the legendary first king of Crete.

other men are concerned. The goals of justice are not to violate our fellow man, and not to offend the rule of modesty. In this we see greatly the power of decorum. Having laid out these general principles, then, and by discussing how we ought to behave, I believe we have now reached an understanding.

[100] The idea of duty, which is drawn from this principle of decorum, has a primary pathway which leads to harmony and the preservation of Nature. If we follow Nature's lead, we will never err. In fact, we will attain following: (1) those things of a sharp and penetrating quality; (2) things which tend to promote sociability among men; and (3) those things which are naturally vigorous and strong. But the greatest power of decorum lies in this part, on which we speak now. The things that are in accordance with Nature must be accommodated, not only where the physical body is concerned, but also with regards to sanctioning the movements of the soul.

[101] The power and nature of the spirit is two-fold: one part resides in the appetite, which in the Greek language is called *orme*. It has the ability to lead a man around this way and that. The other part resides in reason, which teaches and explains what must be done, and what must be avoided. And so it is that when reason is in control, the appetite obeys its commands.

XXIX. Every action ought to be free from rashness and carelessness; and we should never do anything which cannot be traced to a reasonable purpose. This, indeed, is practically a definition of duty.

[102] It must come about that the appetites obey the dictates of reason and that they do not charge blindly ahead. Neither should they lag behind reason due to listlessness or sloth. They should be tranquil and free from all distress of the soul. When this happens, courage and self-control will shine forth brightly. For when appetites wander off a great way on their own and, as it were, enjoy themselves either through lusts or aversions, they are not kept in check by reason, and without doubt exceed all

boundaries and measures. They toss aside reason and leave it behind and do not submit to its influence. But they are still subject to it according to Nature's laws.

Not only are minds disturbed by this sort of thing, but bodies also. One may tell this from looking at the faces of enraged men, or at the faces of those inflamed by passion or fear, or at those craving for some physical delight: the faces, voices, gestures and movements of all of them change profoundly.

[103] It can be concluded from all this—as we turn our attention back to moral duty—that all appetites must be controlled and calmed, and that attention and diligence to this must be paid, so that we do not do something rashly, casually or with frivolity and negligence. We have not been created by Nature for the purpose of playing games or telling jokes; rather, we are here for serious purposes, for great and important pursuits. Of course one may play games and tell jokes, just as we divert ourselves through sleep and other types of rest; but this should happen only when we have first completed our serious and important responsibilities. Along these lines, the manner of joking should not be overly indulgent or immodest, but natural and clever. Just as we do not give children unlimited freedom to amuse themselves but require that they remain within the bounds of proper behavior, so in joking we should let the light of a good character show itself.

[104] There are basically two types of joking. One is ignoble, petulant, disrespectful and obscene; the other is elegant, urbane, witty and facetious. To this second type belong not only our own Plautus and the old Attic comedies, but also the books of the Socratic philosophers.[64] We also have the humorous sayings of many notable men, such as those which have been collected by Cato and called by us *Apophthegmata*. The distinction is simple between a good-natured and a mean-spirited joke. One kind is—

---

[64] By "Attic" Cicero means here Athenian.

if the time is appropriate (i.e., during a time of rest)—worthy of the best sort of man. The other is not worthy of a free man, as it is associated with immoral subject matter and obscene speech.

We must observe the same self-restraint in playing, so that we do not overdo things and, fired up by passion, fall into some kind of indecency. Our campus, and the exertions of the hunt, supply examples of honest types of recreation.[65]

XXX. [105] In all discussions of duty it is important to be mindful of the degree to which the nature of man rises above that of cattle and other beasts of burden. Animals seek nothing except physical pleasure and are sustained in this regard by every impulse. Man, on the other hand, has a mind for learning and pondering things, constantly pursuing his investigations or acting on them. He is carried along by the delight of seeing and hearing. Even if a man has more than a little propensity for physical pleasure, and provided he is not a complete beast (there are some men, alas, who are human only in name), he will, even if caught in the grip of sensual vice, hide and deny his pleasure-seeking behavior out of shame.

[106] From this it can be seen that physical indulgence is unworthy of man's greatness, and it ought to be condemned and rejected. But if we find someone who places a value on such delights, he must hold his enthusiasm diligently within the bounds of reason. Life and growth of the body are traced back to health and strength, not to voluptuary pleasures. If we weigh these matters rationally, and we perceive what is excellent and worthy of our nature as men, we can see how morally wrong it is to dissipate ourselves in luxury, softness and weakness, and how morally right it is to live moderately, frugally, simply and with sobriety.

----

[65]This may refer to the Campus Martius, on which secular games (*ludi saeculares*) were held.

[107] It must be understood that we have been clothed by Nature in a dual character. One of these is held in common by all of us, and which represents the reason and excellence of which we all partake. It is what elevates us above the brutish animals, and from which all moral goodness and decorum are drawn; from this also is derived the way of discovering our responsibilities. The other character, however, is attributed to each person individually.

There are great differences in the types of men. We see some who run with great speed; others who possess the strength for wrestling. And in personal appearance, some have a certain dignity of countenance, while others physical beauty. In souls, too, there are even greater varieties.

[108] Lucius Crassus and Lucius Philippus possessed a great deal of charm; Caius Caesar (Lucius's son) had it also, and used it with greater intensity.[66] In that same era, Marcus Scaurus and Marcus Drusus (the younger) were men of serious purpose.[67] Caius Laelius was a great jokester; his intimate Scipio was a man of great ambition, but led a tragic life. We are told that, among the Greeks, Socrates was pleasant, humorous and jovial in conversation, and a notorious gadfly in his speaking style, which the Greeks call *eirona*. Against this example we have Pythagoras and Pericles, who achieved great heights without using any such lightheartedness. We are informed that Hannibal among the Carthaginians, and Quintus Maximus among our own generals, were cunning and ready to conceal, dissimulate, hide their secrets, set traps for the unwary and anticipate the enemy's plans. In this category the Greeks place Themistocles and Jason of Pherae

---

[66] Lucius Marcus Philippus (141—73 B.C.) was an orator and politician of the republic. He became consul in 91 B.C.

[67] Marcus Livius Drusus was tribune of the plebs in 91 B.C. and was later assassinated.

before other figures.[68] And in the top ranks of cunning and adroit achievements were those of Solon, who pretended to be insane, both to make his life safer, and also to provide a benefit to his country.[69]

[109] But there are also many men who are different from these, honest and open, who believe nothing should be done in secret or by insidious stratagems; they cultivate truth and despise the arts of fraud. Then there are others who will traffic with anyone and endure anything as long as it serves their ultimate goals. Marcus Crassus and Sulla, we observed, were of this sort. We read that Lysander of Sparta was the most devious and patient man of this type; on the other side of the coin was Callicratidas, who was put in command of the fleet after Lysander.

It also happens that, when speaking with others, some men will try to appear as ordinary as any other, even if they possess great power. Such a man was Catulus (both father and son), as well as Quintus Mucius Mancia. When I was young, I heard from older relatives that Publius Scipio Nasica was this sort of man. He was just the opposite of his father, the man who punished Tiberius Gracchus for his pursuit of disastrous policies. His father, indeed, had no such joviality of speech (and neither did Xenocrates, the most austere of philosophers); and for this reason he achieved greatness and lasting fame. Innumerable other variations exist in the natures and habits of men, and we would be remiss in finding fault with them.

XXXI. [110] Indeed everyone must hold tightly to their own particular characteristics—but not their vices—so that decorum, which we are discussing here, may be preserved. We must do

---

[68] Jason of Pherae was the ambitious ruler of Thessaly before the era of Philip II of Macedon. He was assassinated in 370 B.C.

[69] Plutarch (*Solon*, 8) says that Solon feigned insanity by putting on a cap, which was a mark of illness. His goal was to induce the Athenians to renew their efforts at Salamis.

things in such a way that the universal laws of Nature are not violated; and, while preserving those laws, we should follow our own peculiar natures. And although others may be more important and successful, we should still measure our pursuits by the yardstick of our own natures. It is of no use to oppose what Nature herself forbids, and to pursue what one is unable to achieve. From this principle, the decorum of which we earlier spoke emerges even more clearly. As the saying goes, "Nothing is right with a reluctant Minerva, if it is incompatible with Nature and opposed to it."[70]

[111] If decorum is anything, it surely must be nothing more than solid moral consistency through our lives, in every action that we take. This evenness cannot really be maintained if we are imitating other peoples' natures and neglecting our own. Just as we ought to use our own native language—so that we are not mocked as are those who toss around Greek words—so in our actions and in our lives we ought to introduce no type of discordance.

[112] These differences of nature possess such power that sometimes what ought to cause the death of one man, may not cause the death of another man in the same condition. Was not Marcus Cato in one situation, and other men in a different situation, who had surrendered to Caesar in Africa? Perhaps it would have been considered a crime if the others had killed themselves, because their lives had been softer than Cato's and their characters more unsteady. For Cato by nature had an unbelievable seriousness; and this he fortified even more by his steadfast constancy, and by always remaining true to the causes and plans he had taken up. It was his lot to die rather than to gaze on the face of a tyrant.[71]

---

[70] Minerva was the Roman goddess of wisdom. The sentence reads, *Nihil decet invita Minerva, ut aiunt, id est adversante et repugnante natura.*
[71] The "tyrant" referred to here is of course Caesar.

[113] How much did Ulysses suffer in his long wanderings, when he submitted to women (if we can even call Circe and Calypso "women"), while in every statement he wanted to be courteous and congenial to all! At home, he also had to endure the insults of his male and female servants, so that he was eventually able to receive what he wanted.[72] But Ajax, who had his own personality, would have preferred death a thousand times rather than endure this sort of thing. After considering these things, it will be right to judge them in this way: every man ought to deal with the traits he has, and not want to experience those that are more suitable to others. What is most intimately a man's own, is what is most suitable for him.

[114] Everyone, therefore, should get to know his own character, and become a pointed critic of his own virtues and deficiencies. Otherwise, actors may be seen to have more good judgment than do we. Actors do not necessarily choose the best plays, but rather the ones that are most suitable to their skills. Those who rely on their vocal power select the *Epigoni* and the *Medus*; those relying on movement, take the *Melanippa* and the *Clytaemnestra*. I recall that Rupilius always acted in the *Antiope*. Aesopus acted in the *Ajax* less frequently. Should an actor have such good judgment on stage, and a wise man not have it in real life?

We will be most suitable for those things which we are best able to do. But if necessity forces us into something that is not suitable to our nature, all care, thoughtfulness and diligence should be employed, so that we can carry it out, if not with distinction, then with at least as little damage as possible. We do not need to struggle so hard to follow those ideal qualities that

---

[72] Legend says that when Ulysses returned home, he originally disguised himself as a beggar, so that he could assess the situation fully. He found his home filled with assorted parasites and hangers-on, and had to endure their abuse.

have not been given to us; rather, we should struggle to avoid vice.[73]

XXXII. [115] A third type of person can be added to the two types I discussed above. This type is one which accident or occasion sets in place. There is also a fourth, which we accommodate by our own choice. Now kingdoms, empires, noble titles, honors, riches, and influence (as well as their opposites) are dependent on circumstance and governed by chance. How we wish to deal with these factors, however, is a matter of our own personal choice. So some men apply themselves to philosophy, others to the practice of civil law, and still others to the arts of eloquence; and with regard to the virtues, one man may prefer to cultivate one, and another man may prefer another.

[116] For those whose fathers and ancestors won some sort of renown, they themselves are eager to excel in the same activity. This was the case with Quintus Mucius, the son of Publius Mucius, who practiced civil law. It was the same in military affairs with Scipio Africanus, the son of Paulus. To those merits which they inherited from their fathers, these men added something distinctly their own, just as Africanus supplemented his martial glory with eloquence. Timotheus, the son of Colon, who in military achievement was not inferior to his father, to this added learning and cultural refinements. It happens now and then, however, that a few men will disregard the paths of their elders, and follow their own trajectory. They exert themselves considerably and set ambitious goals for themselves, despite coming from obscure origins.

[117] All these questions that we have explored in our search for what is proper should weigh on our minds and our thinking. For we must first decide for ourselves what sort of man we are,

---

[73] I.e., it is better simply to avoid bad things than it is to try to cultivate qualities for which we are ill-suited.

what sort of man we wish to be, and what type of life we want. Of all questions, this one is the most difficult. In adolescence, when the powers of deliberation are at their most feeble, a person decides that his profession should be the thing he loves most at that time. In this way he is entangled in a certain profession and way of life before he is really able to judge what is best for him.

[118] Prodicus says the following about Hercules, which is found in the writings of Xenophon:[74] "When Hercules was approaching maturity, which is the time selected by nature for choosing the road in life one must travel, he sought out an isolated place. Sitting there for a long time, he could not decide which path was better for him. For his could see two paths, one marked 'Pleasure' and another marked 'Virtue.'" This type of thing could perhaps happen to someone like Hercules, "the fruit of the seed of Jove," but not really to us. We follow the guidance of those we have seen, and we are driven forward in life by their example and spirit. For the most part, however, saturated with the worldviews of our parents, we are instructed by their behavior and teachings. Others are carried along by the judgment of the multitude, and opt for what the majority sees as most advantageous. A few, however, whether due to luck or good character, follow the right path in life without having had any parental instruction.

XXXIII. [119] Finally, there is the most rare type. These are the men who, either through superlative ability or incredible erudition and learning, or both, have the opportunity to select at will what path in life they wish to follow. The decision in this regard must hinge on each man's individual character. As was said above, we try to discover what may be appropriate for each man in accordance with his natural-born traits. This principle must

---

[74] Xenophon, *Memorabilia* II.1.21. Prodicus (465-395 B.C.) was a Greek sophist and philosopher. His account of the "choice of Hercules" was a famous teaching story.

be applied continuously in one's entire life as something to be adhered to, so that we can remain true to our natures for our entire lives and not waiver in the performance of our responsibility.

[120] A man's personal nature possesses the greatest power when it comes to the selection of his calling in life. After nature comes Fortune. Each of these is a major factor in choosing the type of life we lead, but Nature's role is more influential. By a significant degree, Nature is more steady, more unchanging: it almost seems that mortal Fortune is carrying on a hopeless contest with immortal Nature. Therefore, he who has constructed his life's plan according to his own vice-free nature, as he ought to do, should hold firmly to this course, unless perhaps he realizes that he has erred in selecting the path he took. If this happens (and it sometimes does), a change in one's life course must be made. If external circumstances help this change, we will do it with more ease and convenience. If external circumstances do not help along such a change, then we must do it in a step-by-step, gradual manner, in the same way that (as wise men tell us) a friendship which no longer pleases us or serves any purpose should be dissolved slowly, rather than terminated suddenly. [121] Changing one's course in life must be undertaken with careful deliberation, so that we may be seen to have done it with due diligence.

Previously, I said that our ancestors ought to be imitated. The first exception to this rule is that their vices should not be emulated. After this, we ought not to imitate something if our personal nature makes us unable to do so. The son of the elder Scipio Africanus (i.e., the man who adopted Scipio the Younger), could not, because of his physical infirmity, match the achievements of his father in the way that Scipio the Younger could be like his own biological father.[75]

If, therefore, a man is unable to try cases in court, or to excel in public speaking, or undertake military campaigns, he still ought to strive for excellence in the virtues within his means—justice, fidelity, generosity, modesty and temperance—so that what is absent from his character may not be so apparent. The best inheritance that can be passed from fathers to their sons—one greater than all other patrimonies—is a reputation for virtue in conducting personal affairs. To disgrace this would be a violation of divine law and must be counted as a sin.

XXXIV. [122] Now because the responsibilities of life are not apportioned evenly among our ages, but are grouped differently in youth and in old age, something also must be said on this variance. It is the duty of youth to respect their elders, to seek out those elders who are the best and most prudent, and to rely on their advice and authority. The ignorance of one's formative years must be fortified and guided by the prudence of old age. Youth absolutely must be protected against wanton sensual indulgence, and hardened in work and discipline in both body and mind, so that it may be fortified for duty in military or civil service. Even when they want to relax and give themselves over to pleasures, let them beware of intemperance, and let them remember modesty. It will be easier to achieve this goal if elders elect to participate in such activities.

––––––––––––––––––––

[75] To understand this sentence we must remember the confusing lineage of the Scipios. Scipio the Younger (Scipio Aemilianus) was one of two biological sons of Lucius Aemilius Paulus Macedonicus. Lucius Aemilius Paulus was a great and famous general, and when he died, his two sons were adopted by prominent families. Scipio the Younger was adopted by Publius Cornelius Scipio. Publius Cornelius Scipio was the eldest biological son of the famous Scipio the Elder (Publius Cornelius Scipio Africanus). When Scipio the Younger was adopted into the famous family of Publius Cornelius Scipio, his official name then became Publius Cornelius Scipio Aemilianus. This describes the connection between Scipio the Elder and Scipio the Younger.

[123] The old, however, should be looking to decrease their physical labor and increasing their mental efforts. They should provide their services to their friends, the youth and most of all to the state, through the rendering of their counsel and prudence. Old age should beware that it does not fall into languor and inactivity. Luxury for any age is scandalous, but in old age it is loathsome. But if intemperance is added to lust, it becomes a two-fold evil: for the same old age thereby adopts disgrace, and also makes the intemperance of the youth more impudent.

[124] It would not be unconnected to our subject at this point to say some words regarding the duties of judges, private parties, citizens and foreigners. It is the duty of a magistrate to bear in mind that he "wears the authority" of the state on his person, and that he ought to uphold its dignity and honor, serve the law and follow legal precedents. He should be ever mindful of the need for fidelity in the discharge of these duties. The private citizen ought to live by right in a fair and equal manner with other citizens, neither submissive nor disenfranchised, and yet also not in an arrogant manner. He should also work to promote concord and tranquility in the state; we ought to feel (and to say) that such a man is a good citizen.

[125] But the business of the foreigner or the foreign resident of a country is to keep to his own concerns; he has no reason to probe into things beyond this and by no means should inject himself into the affairs of his host nation. Thus, in general, duties can be discovered when it is asked what is right for an individual, for various situations, and for different ages. But in carrying out every action and in the execution of a plan nothing is so important as to maintain perseverance.

XXXV. [126] This decorum of which we spoke is discerned in every action, statement and even ultimately in the movement and condition of the body. It is composed of three parts: beauty, order and taste. These concepts are difficult to elucidate, but it will be enough to describe them for our action. In these three elements we find our interest that we be held in high regard by those with whom we live. It is right, then, that we say something on these matters.

Nature seems to have had a grand scheme in the evolution of our physical bodies. Our form and figure generally, as far as its reputable parts are concerned, she has placed in plain view. Those parts given us by Nature for bodily necessities, and that are seen as base and unwholesome, she has set aside and concealed.

[127] The modesty of man follows this artful production of Nature. What Nature hides from public view, all persons of sane mind also keep hidden away; and they take special care to keep such things private. Those parts of the body used for Nature's duties are neither called by their real names, nor are their functions described. It is not immoral to do such things in private, but to speak of them openly is obscene. Thus neither openly doing these things, nor obscenity of speech, is free from immodesty.

[128] Neither should we listen to the Cynics, or to those Stoics who nearly are Cynics, who laugh at us and take us to task, when we consider as shameful the verbal description of deeds that are not immoral, while at the same time verbally describing deeds that are immoral. Piracy, fraud, and adultery are immoral, yet to talk about them is not obscene. To apply oneself to produce children is an honest activity, but to describe it is obscene. Many such things are debated as against modesty with the same sort of sentiment. Let us follow Nature's lead in these matters, then, and let us shun things that are repellent to the eyes and ears. Let this decorum about which we have spoken hold us in our posture, and while walking, sitting or reclining, and in our facial expressions, eyes and hand movements.

[129] There are also two things which should be greatly avoided: that we do not appear effeminate or soft, or that we do not appear rough or too rural. We should not admit that this rule applies to actors and orators but is irrelevant for us. The habit of actors possesses the modesty of traditional discipline, such that no

one would appear for a scene without a loincloth covering. They would fear the possibility that indecent exposure might result if certain parts of the body were revealed. And in our own custom, grown sons do not bathe with their parents, nor do sons-in-law with their fathers-in-law. Therefore, this kind of modesty must be preserved, especially with Nature playing the role of leader and teacher.

XXXVI. [130] There are two type of beauty. One of these is physical attractiveness, and the other is dignity. Physical attractiveness we should consider as belonging to women, and dignity to men. Therefore let unworthy adornments not be displayed on a man's body, and let him likewise beware of this vice in his gestures and movement. Now the movements we see in the palaestra are often disagreeable, and the gestures of actors sometimes show mistakes; but in each type of activity, actions that are correct and simple are praised.[76] Dignity of form must be protected by the excellence of one's physical complexion; the body's good color comes from exercise. Neatness of appearance must be employed not in an annoying or exquisite manner, but in such a way that we dispel any hint of boorishness or uncultured negligence. The same rule should be adhered to with regard to personal dress, in which, as in similar matters, a middle road is optimal.

[131] We must also be on guard lest we move with slowness and excessive looseness in walking; doing so makes us appear like bier-carriers in funeral processions. Neither should we adopt excessive hurrying and running around in a scatter-brained manner. Doing so makes us short of breath; our faces change and our mouths contort. Great significance can be read into this sort of thing, and it erodes our sense of composure. It is of supreme importance to take care that the actions of our souls do not drift

---

[76] The palaestra was a school for wrestling and other athletic activities.

away from the directives of Nature. We will succeed in this if we will be vigilant not to fall into depressions and emotional disturbances, and if we will keep our spirits mindful of the need to preserve dignity.

[132] There are two types of activities of the mind: thinking, and the desires of the appetite. Thinking occupies itself mostly in the seeking of answers; and the appetites impel us to action. Care must therefore be taken that we direct our thinking towards the best things, and submit our appetites to the directives of reason.

XXXVII. The great power of speech comes from two sources: one is public oratory, and the other is private discussion. Oratory is found in disputes before tribunals, in public assemblies, and in the senate; while discussion appears in social circles, private gatherings, meetings of friends and also at large dinners. The rules of oratory are to be found in the study of rhetoric. There are no rules for private discussion, although I fail to see why there could not be. Teachers may be found for students willing to study; but no one embarks on a study of conversation. Yet we always see packed crowds before rhetoricians! The rhetorical principles governing words and sentences in oratory apply equally to private conversation.

[133] Since we have the voice as the messenger of speech, we ought to seek two qualities with regard to the voice: clarity and smoothness. Each of these qualities must be sought from Nature. Practice will improve clarity; as for the other, deliberate imitation of those who speak eloquently and smoothly is advisable. There was nothing in the Catuli that might make you believe that they had exquisite judgment in letters, even though they were erudite.[77]

---

[77] The Catuli were prominent members of the Roman aristocracy who featured in some of Cicero's works (e.g., *De oratore.*). Quintus Lutatius Catulus (the Elder) was consul with Caius Marius in 102 B.C. He is known to have married Domitia, the sister of Gnaeus Domitius, who was tribune in 104 B.C.

There were many others of this type, and yet the Catuli were thought to be the very best in the use of the Latin language. Their elocution was pleasant, their words were neither artificial nor overwhelming, and neither obscure nor pedantic; their voices were without tension, yet neither sluggish nor ringing. The more fertile speech of Lucius Crassus was not less clever, but the Catuli's reputation for wonderful speech is no less than his. In salt and wit Caesar, the brother of Catulus (through a common father), truly dominated everyone. In forensic oratory he defeated the arguments of others with his own style of speaking.

Therefore, if we are exerting ourselves in pursuit of all these things, we should inquire into the basic principles that I have outlined above.

[134] Conversation, in which the Socratics excel, should be smooth and contain little that is pertinacious; it should also possess humor. Let him who would enter into a conversation not exclude others, so that when others participate, he does not think that a change in the conversation's flow is unfair. Let him first see what the topic of conversation is, and what is being spoken about. If it is a serious matter, let him adhere to a serious subject; if a humorous subject, let him be witty. Most vitally, let him take care that the conversation does not reveal some vice of character. This most often happens when malicious slanders are readily spoken (whether jokingly or seriously) against people who are not present.

[135] The majority of serious conversations are about domestic affairs, politics, and the pursuits of the arts and education. Effort must be made, if the conversation begins to stray into unrelated matters, to steer it back on course (to the degree that

---

His son (Catulus the Younger) was Quintus Lutatius Catulus Capitolinus; he was consul at a different time. The elder Catulus died in 87 by his own hand, on the direction of Marius.

those present can accept it). We are not stimulated by the same things at all times in a similar way. We must also be aware that, to the extent a conversation produces pleasure and had a valid reason to start, it must also be broken off in a like-minded way.

XXXVIII. [136] But just as we are most correctly instructed in other aspects of life, that we should avoid emotional disturbances (i.e., emotional outbursts not controlled by reason), so should we aim to avoid such things in our conversations. Let there be no anger, cupidity, laziness, sloth or anything of this sort. The greatest care must also be taken that we are seen to value and respect those with whom we are conversing.

Sometimes delivering rebukes to others may be necessary. In such situations perhaps a harsh voice and pointed words may be brought to bear, so that we may appear to be angry. This sort of castigation should come rarely and against our will as a last resort, just as the cutting and cauterization of a limb is a last resort to the doctor when all else has failed. Even so, let true anger always be absent: for nothing good can come from anger, and certainly nothing well-advised.

[137] In most situations a lenient reprimand is permitted in a way that, joined with seriousness, severity is employed while offensive language is avoided. When a reproof is joined with harshness, it should be demonstrated that such methods were undertaken for the sake of the person being reprimanded. It is better in these types of discussions (even if they are with our enemies), to retain our composure and suppress our rage if we are subjected to insults. Those things that happen as a result of emotional perturbation can neither be done with a clear mind, nor with the approval of those present. It is also disgraceful to preach arrogantly about oneself--particularly if the things said are false-- and, to the mockery of those listening, to take on the role of the

"boastful soldier."[78]

XXXIX. [138] Since we are probing into these matters in great detail, we should want to follow up on one more. It must be asked what sort of living quarters a man of importance and station should possess. Its focus should be on utility; its plan of construction should be geared towards this. Care must also be taken for convenience and quality. We heard that Gnaeus Octavius, who was the first from that family to have been made consul, built a wonderful and sumptuous house on the Palatine; it was seen by many of the common crowd, and apparently helped him (a "new man") get elected to the consulship. But Scaurus demolished the house on his own accession, and annexed the land to his own holdings.[79] Thus he, Gnaeus Octavius, brought into his house his family's first consulship; but the other man, Scaurus, the son of a great and most honorable figure, brought to his own renovated house not only electoral defeat, but utter disgrace and calamity.

[139] One's dignity may be on display in one's house, but a house cannot provide everything. It is the master who must decorate the house, and not the other way around. As in many such things, a man must think not only of himself, but also of others; the house of an important man must be capable of accommodating

---

[78] In Roman drama, especially in the comedic plays of Plautus, there were certain stock characters that appeared over and over. Some of these were: the clever and subtle slave, the kind-hearted prostitute, and the boastful soldier. The boastful soldier was a bore who never stopped talking about his achievements, whether real or exaggerated.

[79] Marcus Aemilius Scaurus (163—89 B.C.) was a highly respected Roman politician who was elected consul in 115 B.C. He had a son with the same name and it is this Scaurus who is referred to here. The younger Scaurus was backed by the First Triumvirate for political office, but was accused of extortion in Sardinia. He was defended by Cicero and acquitted. Cicero, we can see clearly here, had no illusions about his client's culpability.

many guests and visitors of different sorts, and should therefore be sufficiently capacious. On the other hand, a large house becomes a discredit to its owner if it has the feel of solitude, especially if it used to be visited often when it had a different owner. It certainly is offensive when passers-by say the following:

O ancient dwelling! How different
Is the new master who here resides![80]

Indeed, in these times, one may apply this saying to many different houses.

[140] Care must be taken (especially if you are building your own house) that you do not exceed reasonableness when it comes to expense and splendor. This is the source of much evil, as we have noted in the quote above. Many people in this regard eagerly imitate the actions of important persons. But who imitates the virtues of Lucius Lucullus, that most excellent man?[81] And yet how many tried to imitate his incredible houses! Some limit should be imposed on such things, in order to regain some basic standard of moderation. Likewise, this same sense of moderation ought to be transferred to the conduct of all aspects of our personal lives.

But let us move on to a different topic.

[141] In every action undertaken, three things must be adhered to: *first*, that our appetite submits itself to reason (for nothing is more conducive to carrying out one's duties than this); *second*, that we take notice of the effort we will need to expend, so that we expend neither too much nor too little energy than the case requires. The *third* principle is that we take care to control those

---

[80] These lines are from some iambic *senarii*, but there are words missing. A *senarius* is a Latin verse of six feet. The poet is unknown.

[81] Lucius Licinius Lucullus (118—57 B.C.) was a general and politician closely associated with the dictator Sulla.

things that pertain to the bearing and dignity of a gentleman. The best way to grasp this same honor is to employ ways we have described above, and not to depart too far from this. Of these three principles, however, the most important is to condition the appetite to obey reason.

XL. [142] Finally, we must say something regarding the order of things and the suitability of occasions. These subjects are contained in that term which the Greeks call *eutaxin*. It is not that word which we interpret as "moderation" (which has the same derivation); but rather we mean the word *eutaxia*, that is, the preservation of order. Therefore let us similarly call it moderation, as it is defined by the Stoics. Moderation is knowing how to assign those things that are said or done to their proper place.

Thus, the "ordering" and the "correct assignment" of things are basically the same. They define "order" in this way: the right arrangement of things, in their right places. By place of action, however, they really mean advantageousness of situation. The right advantage of situation is called in Greek *eukairia*, and in Latin *occasio*. Thus it may be, that this "moderation" (as we interpret it and as I have explained), is simply the skill of knowing how to do the right action in the right situation.

[143] But the definition of prudence is the same, as I related at the outset of this study. At this point in our discussion, however, we are trying to discover the nature of moderation and temperance and of virtues similar to these. Those virtues relevant to prudence have already been discussed in their suitable places. Those subjects connected to the virtues on which we have been speaking for some time now—those which relate to modesty and respect, and with which we interact daily—at this point must be discussed.

[144] This, therefore, is the order of action that must be used so that, in the same way a speech is well-constructed, all things in a man's life may be balanced and in proportion. For it is disgraceful and extremely rude, when a serious subject is being dealt with, to toss about the kind of frivolous table-talk that is

more suitable for an informal gathering. This point is well-illustrated in the following story. Pericles had the famous poet Sophocles as his colleague in the praetorship and they both held joint responsibility for command. An attractive boy once walked by them both. Sophocles said to Pericles, "What a handsome young lad, Pericles!" But Pericles responded, "A good praetor, Sophocles, ought to be abstinent not only with his hands, but also with his eyes."

But if Sophocles had said this, for example, at a training gym for athletes, he would have been fairly free from reprimand. Such is the authority given by place and time! If a man is about to undertake a court case and rehearses it to himself while on a journey or while walking, or if he is pondering some matter with a great deal of attentiveness, no one should fault him. But if he were to do the same thing at a formal dinner, he would be seen as disrespectful in his ignorance of the occasion.

[145] But those things that deviate the most from proper gentility, like singing in the market-place or some other type of bizarre perversity, are easily noticed. They do not usually merit overt admonition or a specific teaching point. However, what are considered "minor" sins, indistinguishable from the many other actions we do, must still be more diligently culled out from our other actions. Even if a harp or flute is out of tune only a little bit, it will still be noticed by the practiced ear. So we must be vigilant in life, lest something by chance be out of alignment. In fact we should be more vigilant, since harmony in life resides much more and much better in actions than in musical notes.

XLI. [146] So, just as the sensitive ear listening to the harp can distinguish the smallest subtlety, so we, if we wish to be sharp and diligent in detecting vices, will conclude much information from small things. From a look in the eyes, from the abating and furrowing of the eyebrows, from sadness, cheerfulness and laughter, from speech, silence, or in the raising or lowering of the voice, and from other such indicators from people, we can easily judge what is right and what departs from duty and Nature. And in order to decide which of our actions is troublesome to others, it behooves us to watch for how other people react. What others find annoying, we should avoid. For it often happens (I know not how) that we discern more easily the faults of others than those in ourselves. Students are improved more easily when a teacher actually demonstrates vices for the sake of teaching a lesson to his pupils.

[147] It is also not unheard of, when duties must be chosen that raise doubts in our minds, to consult with learned or skilled men, from whom such inquiries may prove useful. The majority of men, in fact, is accustomed to be carried along passively as their own natures incline them. One must examine not only what someone says, but also what he actually feels, and also for what reason he feels that way. For just as painters, sculptors and poets want to have their works reviewed by the public, so that what the public finds wanting may be corrected, and just as the artists themselves and their confidants examine their works to see what needs fixing, so very much through hearing the judgment of others should we determine what should be done and should not be done, and what should be corrected, and what should be changed.

[148] Nothing need be taught about those things that are done through custom and civil institutions. These things are in fact rules themselves. And no one ought to be led to believe that, just because Socrates or Aristippus said or did something against tradition or civil customs, he himself may venture to do the same. These men acquired this special license by virtue of their unique and divine qualities. The entire doctrinal system of the Cynics, to be sure, must be thrown out: it is hostile to good sense, without which nothing can be morally right, and nothing honorable.

[149] We also ought to heed and imitate those who have demonstrated a life of honesty and greatness, those who have served their countries well and continue to do so, just as if they were invested with some honor or office. We ought also to grant

much deference to old age, and to defer to those who hold magisterial offices. We should be mindful of the difference between a citizen and a foreigner, and in the case of the foreigner, whether he arrived of his own accord or in an official capacity. To sum up—and for fear of elevating one point over the others—we ought to preserve, protect and cultivate the union and association of all groups of men.

XLII. [150] Now we turn to craftsmen and other types of occupations, to see which ones are gentlemanly and which ones are vulgar. These general guidelines will apply. The first occupations which incur our disapproval are those which tend to incur the wrath of others, such as tax-collectors and moneylenders. Unworthy and sordid also are all employments of hired labor, who are paid by the job and not by their talents. Their salaries are nothing but the wages of servitude. Lowly also are those who buy goods from merchants and then sell them at once for a profit; such profiteers really do nothing, except misrepresent to a high degree. Nothing is so foul as this sort of manipulation. All run-of-the-mill workmen are basically vulgar, for no workshop can really have anything noble about it. We should least of all value those trades that serve the sensual pleasures:

Fish-sellers, butchers, cooks, poulterers, and fishermen,

As the playwright Terence tells us.[82] To these jobs may also be added, if we wish, the dealers of perfumes or ointments, dancers and all participants in the *ludus talarius*.[83]

---

[82] *Eunuchus* II.26.

[83] The *ludus talarius* seems to have been some sort of staged dance performance or pantomime. It may also have had another incarnation as a game of dice (*talus* means both *ankle* and *dice*). The rhetorician Quintilian (II.3.58) mentions it as a sort of freewheeling musical dance show. Such performances

[151] Of those trades that require a high degree of skill, and no small amount of intelligence, we find medicine, architecture, and teaching; these professions are most respectable for those who achieve them. Commerce, if it is of the small-business type, is considered sordid. But if it is a large and extensive business enterprise, importing much from everywhere and distributing goods without dishonesty, it must not be criticized too much. And if the merchant is satisfied with his profits, or rather content with them--for as often as he brings goods from the sea into port, so he brings his possessions to his private estates--commerce can rightly be praised as the best sort of work.

But of all the things from which one can extract gain, nothing is better than agriculture, nothing more productive, nothing more pleasant, and nothing more worthy of a free man. Because we have already spoken on this subject at length in my treatise *Cato Maior*, you may find there the necessary illustrations of this point.[84]

XLIII. [152] Regarding these divisions which make up moral goodness, and in what way duties are derived from them, we have said enough. But with regard to morally upright actions, a tension and balancing can occur with regard to which one is more moral: this was a point unfortunately missed by Panaetius. Now since all moral rightness comes from four sources (the first of which is *critical thinking*, the second *community*, the third *generosity of spirit*, and the fourth *moderation*), it is necessary in selecting the right duty that these sources be compared with each other.

[153] Therefore, those duties which come from one's

---

were traditionally looked down on by the Roman elite, as they were seen as lewd and unbecoming for decent women.

[84] Cicero's *Cato Maior De senectute* (usually referred to simply as *De senectute*, or *On Old Age*) contains a digression in praise of agriculture (XV.51). Cato himself also wrote an extant treatise on agriculture (*De agri cultura*).

community are more in accordance with Nature than those which come from analysis.[85] This can be confirmed by the following argument. Imagine that a man had sufficient wisdom that he was awash in a tidal wave of abundance, to the extent that he might consider, and ponder with the greatest leisure, all those things worth thinking about. Yet if his solitude were such that he could not see another human being, he would perish. The most important of all virtues is wisdom, which the Greeks call *sophia*. Prudence, which they call *phronesis*, we believe to be something else: it is the knowledge of those things we should seek out, and of those things we should avoid.

This wisdom, of which I have spoken as a first principle, consists of both human and divine knowledge. It embraces the community of gods and men, and the fellowship between them. If wisdom is all-important (as it certainly is), we must conclude that the duty arising from one's community is the most important type of duty.[86] Indeed, the analysis and contemplation of Nature might be feeble and incomplete, if no firm action were to follow from such cogitations. This type of action is chiefly discerned in the protection of men's interests. It therefore applies vitally to human society and must be placed before analytical thought.

[154] All the best men point this out and concur on its truth. For who is so obsessed with observing and studying the universe that he would not drop and abandon everything, if suddenly dangers and crises arose for his country and he was able to provide relief or render aid? Even if he were examining and thinking about some worthy subject? And even if he were counting the stars or measuring the size of the world? The same could be said about our parents or about a dear friend, if they were faced with danger.

[155] We are to understand from all of this the following: the

---

[85] I.e., those which come as a result of thinking or investigation.
[86] I.e., duties arising from social obligations.

duties of justice must come before the pursuit of knowledge and its associated activities. The duties of justice relate to the life of man and nothing is more venerable than this.

XLIV. And yet those same men, whose entire lives have revolved around the activities of the mind, have not failed to answer the call to add to the benefits and advantages of mankind. They have trained many men to be better and more productive citizens in the affairs of their countries. So the Pythagorean Lysis mentored Epaminondas the Theban, and Plato taught Dion the Syracusan.[87] And indeed there are many other examples of this. We ourselves, whatever we may have contributed to our own country—if indeed we have contributed anything—we accomplished with the assistance of our teachers and the instructed wisdom with which they filled us.

[156] Not only do such men instruct and teach willing students while they are alive and present, but they continue to do so after their deaths by virtue of the literary monuments which they leave behind. They have missed no point dealing with the laws or customs relevant to political theory to such an extent that they seem to have contributed all their leisure time for our advantage. Through their devotion to instruction and dedication to knowledge, these same men bring their most acute prudence and intelligence to the general benefit of humanity. For this reason also, well-equipped speech, sensibly directed, is better than the sharpest thinking bereft of eloquence. For thinking is a self-directed activity, while eloquence embraces those others with whom we share our social community.

[157] And just as a swarm of bees does not collect together for the purpose of creating goodwill, but rather they create

---

[87] Dion of Syracuse (408—354 B.C.) was tyrant of the city of Syracuse in Sicily and a student of Plato. Lysis of Taras (fl. 5th cent. B.C.) was a philosopher said to have been trained by Pythagoras. He eventually made his way to Thebes and mentored Epaminondas.

honeycomb as a consequence of their natural sociability, so men also (and to a much greater extent) congregate naturally, and bring to bear their collective resourcefulness in thinking and acting. Unless true virtue, which watches over mankind (i.e., the whole of human society), infuses itself into the investigation of human affairs, such investigation will remain nothing but cold and barren cogitation.

Similarly, greatness of soul which is improperly connected with human society and kinship may become a kind of barbarity and savagery.[88] Thus it must be that man's social bonds, and the interests of human society, are to be placed before the pursuit of knowledge.

[158] It is not true, as some say, that these social bonds exist for the sake of life's necessities. Without the aid of others we might not be able to take care of the things required by Nature, and enter into the community and society of our fellow man. But if all of us were supplied with food and shelter by some sort of "magic wand" (as they call it), then the best men among us could neglect his proper business, and occupy himself entirely in study and thought.

This would not happen, of course. Such a man would flee from solitude and seek a companion for his studies; he would want to learn and to teach, to listen and to speak. Therefore, every duty which tends to promote the social bonds among men and protect their integrity must be placed *before* a duty which concerns itself with mental investigation and abstract knowledge.

---

[88] This sentence and the previous one are profound. Cicero is saying that human thought (including scientific thought) must be grounded in, and guided by, moral considerations. He also calls our attention to the fact that "greatness of soul" (*magnitudo animi*, an elusive phrase which approximately means having a courageous or expansive spirit) is useless unless it is connected to our social fabric. In other words, both cold calculation and courage are nothing unless they have a social conscience. Modern science would do well to revisit these passages for ethical guidance.

XLV. [159] Perhaps a relevant question should be asked here. Should this sense of community, which is the most suitable from Nature's perspective, always be placed before the virtues of modesty and moderation? The answer must be no. There are some things that are so repellent, and so immoral, that even a wise man trying to save his country would not do them. The philosopher Posidonius has catalogued a number of such acts; but some of them are so foul and obscene that even talking about them would look immoral. The prudent man will not do such things for the sake of his country, nor will his country wish such actions to be undertaken for its sake. In the event, this is not really an issue, since situations do not arise when it is important for the state to have a wise man do these sorts of things.

[160] In sum, we must consider the matter settled: in choosing between duties, the type of duty that is more important is the one that tends to hold together human society. For deliberated action follows from thinking and prudence; and to do something in a well-considered way is worth more than crafty deliberation alone.

So much, then, for this subject. Our review has demonstrated that it is not difficult to see, in investigating a duty, which one should be given priority. In any community there are levels of duties, from which we can discern the following gradations: *first*, to the immortal gods; *second*, to our country; *third*, to our parents; and *lastly*, to those remaining as they ought to be rendered.

[161] From this brief analysis given above, we can appreciate that men not only often doubt what is moral or immoral, but also, when presented with two moral propositions, which one may be more moral than the other. As I noted previously, this was a point missed by Panaetius. But let us continue with the remainder of our discussion.

COMMENTARY ON BOOK I

The first book lays out the general framework of the discussion and sets the tone for the rest of the treatise. The subject matter, of course, is the identification and description of one's proper duties. Ethics and morals are inherently implicated. These two terms may be not be precisely the same thing, but they certainly overlap. According to the Oxford English Dictionary (1969 ed.), ethics are "the moral principles by which a person is guided" or "the rules of conduct recognized in certain associations or departments of human life." The same dictionary's entry for "moral" states that Cicero himself invented its present meaning, and from him the word passed into the Romance and Teutonic languages. We know this from a passage in his fragmentary treatise *De fato* (*On Fate*).[89] Morals pertain to "character or disposition, considered as good or bad, virtuous or vicious…[or to] the distinction between right and wrong, or good and evil, in relation to actions, volitions, or character of responsible beings."[90]

Cicero acknowledges his predecessor Panaetius in I.3 but makes it clear that he intends to correct his shortcomings. Instead of Panaetius's threefold classification of duties, Cicero tells us

---

[89] The key sentence is the broken opening line of *De fato* I.1: …*quia pertinet ad mores, quod "ethos" illi vocant, nos eam partem philosophiae de moribus appellare solemus, sed decet augentem linguam Latinam, nominare moralem.* ("Because it relates to personal characteristics, which they call ethos; we usually call that part of philosophy the study of character. But it is right to add to the Latin language by calling this 'morals.'")

[90] OED (1969 ed.) entry for "moral."

that there really should be five. Where he builds on Panaetius is in the matter of relative merits and conflicts. What happens when we are faced with two "morally correct" choices? How can we tell which one is more "right" than the other? And what happens when we have two choices that are "advantageous," and then need to decide which of the two is more advantageous?

In I.5, he lays out the four sources of moral rectitude (the terms "moral goodness" and "moral rectitude" are interchangeable). It is important to pay attention to these, as they will figure later in the treatise. He also introduces other concepts that will be given detailed treatment later: good faith as the cornerstone of justice (I.7), the folly of ambition (I.8), and how changes in external conditions can justify a breach of duties (I.10).

Also significant is Cicero's grounding of his concept of duties on a "natural" ethic. Man is, according to Nature, a social animal, and must get along with his peers in order for society to have any chance of success (I.16). Here we have confirmation of Cicero's emphasis of the practical side of things. He does not exhort us necessarily to do good for abstract reasons. Rather, the reasons for following one's duties lie in the social bonds that every man has with his fellow man. These duties may vary according to circumstances (I.18) but some sort of duty will always exist.

Anthropologists here confirm what Cicero says. Morals may vary from time and place and from society to society; in a narrow sense they can thus be said to be "relative." But this certainly does not mean that morals are worthless. Their relativity only proves their flexibility and resilience as to time and place. Every society has had them and every society needs them. They are products of human social activity and are the glue that hold us all together.

The concept of "greatness of spirit" (*magnitudo animi*) makes its appearance in I.19—I.20 and is of critical significance. It may be the most important theme running through the entire work. Besides serving a purpose in binding us to our fellow man, moral duties elevate us closer to divine virtues like fortitude, patriotism and service. A great and noble spirit has two features: (1) it will be contemptuous of the baser things of this world, and (2) it will seek to challenge itself through arduous activities.

Another important concept introduced is the idea that we must do those things which are best suited to us (I.31). What may be good for one man may not be right for another, and it does us no good to try to compete with someone else on this level. This leads directly into his discussion of career choices. Cicero closes the first book with a brief discussion of justice and how we can give duties some sort of "ranking." (I.45).

Although he recognizes the debt that society owes to scholars for their contributions to knowledge, Cicero makes it clear that knowledge unmoored to a sense of justice will do us more harm than good. Knowledge without the tempering influence of justice is immoral and base in the same way that courage without restraint can degenerate into savagery (I.44). Human society must always take priority over the selfish needs of individuals. And on this profound note, the first book ends.

BOOK II: ADVANTAGEOUSNESS

Book II

I. [1] Marcus, my son, I believe in the preceding book we have fully explained both how duties are drawn from moral goodness and, in addition, the different types of virtue. From this point, I intend to evaluate the types of duties that relate to a civilized life, and the means men use to acquire such a life, as well as resources and wealth. As I have already said, the question here is: what is advantageous, and what is not advantageous? And of several advantageous choices, what is a better than average choice, and what is the best one? I will now enter into a discussion of these matters. Before doing this, I will say a few words regarding my general purpose and point of view.

[2] Although my books have stimulated more than a few people with the desire not only to read, but also to write, I still sometimes fear that the name "philosophy" might be resented by some good men. They may wonder why I spend so much of my labor and time in such pursuits.

While the state was governed by those to whom it had attached itself, I directed all my energy and thinking to it. But when everything came to be held under the control of one man, there was no longer any real place for my advice or authority.[91] When I lost my colleagues who were tasked with guarding the republic—men of great distinction—I did not give in to anguish,

---

[91] Cicero is here referring to Julius Caesar and his (in Cicero's view) unjust takeover of the state. He could see little in Caesar besides a destroyer of republican institutions. But he could not see that Caesar, or a man like him, was made inevitable by a generation of civil war and social turmoil.

as I might well have done, but rather resisted these feelings. Neither did I take refuge in sensual pleasures, which are unworthy of a learned man.

[3] How I wish that the republic had stood firm in the political stance it had taken, and had not crossed paths with those men who were eager not so much to reform institutions, but to overturn them! For one thing, when I used to be occupied in politics, my efforts were more focused on political affairs than on writing. I would not be here transcribing my philosophical essays, but rather my public orations, as I used to do. And when the republic in which I placed all cares, thoughts, and works was altogether dissolved, the courts fell silent, as did my voice in the senate-chamber.

[4] As I was unable to occupy my mind with former activities, I turned to those studies that I had undertaken in my early years and that I thought would be a worthy way of soothing my troubles. I drew myself once again to philosophy. As a youth I had spent a good deal of time in learning philosophy; and after I began to enter a political career and was devoting myself completely to public service, there was only so much time for philosophy as was left over after the time I needed for work and my friends. Even this was completely consumed in reading; there was no leisure for writing.

II. [5] Nevertheless, out of these great evils something good has followed. I commit my doctrines to written form here. They are not very well-known to the public, but most worthy of being known. For what, by God, is more worth learning than wisdom? What is most outstanding, or better for a man, or more worthy? Those who seek wisdom are called philosophers; and philosophy itself is really nothing more—if you want it to be defined—than the study of wisdom. Wisdom, however, as it was defined by the old-school philosophers, is the knowledge of human and divine matters and of the causes which sustain them. And if someone should criticize the study of philosophy as something pointless, I would like to know what he believes to be worth praising.

[6] Now if one seeks the pleasures of the mind and a release from worldly cares, what can compare with the studies of men who probe into those philosophical questions that point to and validate a good life? But if reason is directed by constancy and virtue, then either this is the method by which we achieve wisdom, or there is no method at all. To say that there is no method for analyzing the greatest of things,[92] when there is no minor thing without some method, is the talk of unreflective men and of men who err in the issues that matter most in life. If indeed there were some way of learning virtue, and if one has abandoned this type of study, where else may it be sought?

These considerations steer us towards philosophy. They have been dealt with more extensively elsewhere, when I discussed them in another of my books. In the present context it is sufficient for me to say that, having been deprived of my public office, I directed my energy to this most important avocation.

[7] It happens to me on occasion that I hear learned and erudite men asking: are you consistent enough in your ideas? Although we say that nothing can be known for certain, we are nevertheless often ready to offer opinions on various matters; at the same time, we are attempting to lay out the rules of duties.[93] In this regard I wish our way of thinking to be clearly understood. We are not like those whose minds wander in error and have nothing of substance in them. What kind of frame of mind, or rather what kind of life, would we have if we were deprived of reason not only in discourse, but also in living? There are thinkers who say that some things are certain and other things uncertain. We, however, respectfully dissent from this view: *we say that some things are probable and others less so.*

---

[92] I.e., wisdom and philosophy.

[93] Cicero was a member of the so-called "New Academy", which adhered to a skeptical and eclectic view of philosophy: nothing could be known for certain.

112

[8] So what prevents me from following what seems to me probable, and rejecting what is improbable, and avoiding the assertions of arrogance in order to steer clear of rashness, which separates many from true wisdom? In response to those who say that we dispute everything, I say: we do this because it is not possible to reveal what is probable, unless a comparison of various causes has been made from each different perspective.

But this has already been explained fully, I believe, in my treatise *Academics*. You, my Cicero, although you are immersing yourself in the most ancient and noble philosophy of the master Cratippus—who is similar to those great men who originally founded his school—I still would not want my own school, which is so similar to yours, to be unknown to you. Let us proceed with the main lines of our discussion.

III. [9] Five rational principles have been proposed for the pursuance of moral duties. Two of them pertain to honor and integrity. Two pertain to the conveniences of life: that is, resources, influence and ability. The fifth pertains to the selection of the right moral duty, if any of the ones I listed above are found to be in conflict with each other. The section on moral goodness has been completed,[94] and this is the section in which I want you to be most well-versed.

The subject that we now move into is what is known as "advantageousness."[95] The meaning of this word has become corrupted, and its usage gradually warped. Things have reached a point where, in trying to distinguish moral goodness from advantageousness, people believe that something may have moral rectitude without having expediency, and expediency without any

---

[94] In the first book, where moral goodness was discussed in detail.

[95] The word here is *utile*, which can be rendered as expediency, advantageousness, or utility. To avoid monotony in the text I interchange these terms as needed, just as *honestas* can be interchangeably rendered as moral goodness or moral rectitude.

moral goodness. Nothing more insidious than this could be introduced into the moral life of man.

[10] Indeed, philosophers of the most eminent authority distinguish plainly and honestly between these three blended ways of thinking. They believe that whatever is just is also expedient; and whatever is morally good is also just. We can conclude from this, then, that whatever is morally good is also expedient. Those who have not reflected on these things deeply enough (i.e., those who admire scheming and cunning men) often judge deviousness to be wisdom. This type of error must be eradicated, and every such opinion must be brought to the realization that the things such people want cannot be attained by either wickedness or fraud.

[11] With regard to the things needed to support life, some of them are inanimate, such as gold, silver, and the products drawn from the earth. Some of them are also animate, and have their own mental impulses and controlling appetites. Of these, some are lacking in reason, and some make use of it. Deficient in reason are horses, cows, and the remaining types of domesticated animals, as well as bees; but by their works, things are produced for the use and life of man. Of the types of beings that use reason, philosophers tell us that there are two: gods and men. Piety and a sanctified character work to placate the gods. After the gods, man can provide the greatest benefit to his fellow man.

[12] We have the same categorization for the things that irritate us, or are harmful to us. But because some people think that the gods do not hurt us, they pay them no mind, and judge that men are mostly harmful to other men. Regarding those things that we have above called inanimate, we should remember that they have mostly been produced by man. We would not have such things, but for the intervention of human arts and labor. Neither would we enjoy them without man's administration. Without the diligent labors of man there would be no medical treatment, navigation, agriculture or the harvesting and storing of produce and growing crops.

[13] And, as a matter of fact, there would also be no exporting of those things in which we abound, and no importation of those things which we lack, if men were not engaged in these duties. For the same reason, the stone needed for human use would not be quarried from the earth, nor would "iron, copper, gold, silver, buried deeply" ever be excavated without the labor and cleverness of man.[96]

IV. If not for the shared community life of man, which taught men to seek mutual help for necessities, how would we have roofs that keep out the cold and alleviate the effects of heat; roofs that early man was able to give to his fellows and afterwards to maintain in the face of storms, earthquakes, and the decay that would collapse them? [14] Consider also the aqueducts, the dredged canals, the agricultural irrigation systems, the moles, and the man-made harbors: would we have these things but for the labor of man?[97] It can be seen from these and many other examples that we would in no way have been able to enjoy the benefits and profits of such inanimate things had it not been for the labor and application of man.

Finally, how could the use and benefit of animals ever be gained without the help of mankind? Man was certainly the prime mover in discovering what beasts could be domesticated, and to what use they could be put. In our own day, without man's labor, we would not be able to feed them, train them, protect them or take what is best from them. Similarly, man kills those animals which cause harm, and captures those which he is able to make use of.

---

[96] The quoted phrase is believed to be from the tragic poet Lucius Accius (170—c. 86 B.C.) in his work *Prometheus*. He may have been imitating line 580 of the *Prometheus* of Aeschylus. Cicero apparently met him personally (*Brutus* 72-73).

[97] A mole is a structure on the water's edge that serves as a pier, breakwater, or causeway. It can also refer to the artificial harbor created by such a structure.

[15] Do we even need to list all the various types of fine arts, without which we could hardly have a life at all? Who could be rescued from sickness? What enjoyment would there be for the healthy? Who could be nourished or refined, if the many fine arts did not attend to us? From all this it is clear that the enriched life of man is distant from the life and lot of the animals. Without the assembled organization of people, cities would not have been able to be constructed or populated, from which laws and customs were instituted. Then came the equal distribution of laws, and a certain custom of living. From these things followed a clemency of spirit towards others, and a binding social respect, so that life became more secure. And by giving and accepting goods and services, we were thus lacking in nothing.

V. [16] We have lingered on this issue rather more than is necessary. For whom are these things (which have been discussed at length by Panaetius) not clear? No one, either as a leader in war or in civilian affairs, can do great and beneficial things without the enthusiastic participation of other men. He recounts the careers of Themistocles, Pericles, Cyrus, Agesilaus and Alexander; and he refutes the assertion that their deeds could have been accomplished without the help of other men. To prove his point, however, he makes use of unnecessary testimonial evidence.

And although we find tremendous benefits in the joint efforts and consensus of man, at the same time there is no more detestable pestilence than that which is brought down upon man by his fellow man. There is a book by Dicaearchus which talks about the ruin of man.[98] He was a great and prolific Peripatetic who collected together various causes of ruin, such as floods, pestilences, devastations, and sudden attacks by swarms of wild

---

[98] Dicaearchus of Messana (c.350—285 B.C.) was a Greek philosopher, mathematician, and geographer. *See* Cicero, *De legibus* III.6.

animals. He alleges that such occurrences nearly consumed whole groups of humans; but then he contrasts this with how many more men have been destroyed by their fellows, such as in wars and revolutions, and that this number far exceeds those destroyed by natural causes.

[17] Since there can be no doubt on this point—that man is to his fellow man both the greatest help and the greatest harm—I say that the special characteristic of virtue is *the winning over of the hearts of men and the joining of them together in one's useful purpose*. The benefits accruing to human life derived from inanimate things, and from the use and treatment of animals, we designate as the laborious arts; and the devotions of men who are ready and willing to improve our common situation, are awakened by the wisdom and virtue of the most outstanding personalities.

[18] As a matter of fact, all virtue generally hinges on three aspects. The *first* is the ability to perceive what is true and genuine, what something may be in harmony with, what can follow from something, and what things may be produced by something else. The *second* is the ability to restrain mental distress, which the Greeks call *pathe*, as well as the appetites (which they call *hormas*), by making them obedient to reason. The *third* aspect is to make use of moderation and knowledge, so that (a) we may be satisfied and fulfilled in the pursuit of those things required by Nature; (b) we may be able to drive away something harmful introduced into our lives; and (c) we may avenge ourselves on those who try to hurt us and inflict such punishment as may be consistent with equity and humanity.

VI. [19] We will discuss those principles by which we are able to secure the ability to win and hold men's devotions. But a few words must first be said on some preliminary matters.

Who cannot know the great power that Fortune wields in granting the things we desire on the one hand, and in sending adversities our way on the other? We enjoy Her when She sends us a propitious gust of wind, and we are carried to our desired landing. But when She blows again, we are destroyed. Fortune does, however, have more rare incidents, such as those impersonal ones: storms, hurricanes, shipwrecks, disasters and fires, and from animals, kicks, bites and attacks. These, as I have said, are infrequent.

[20] But recall the destruction of armies (which recently happened to three of them,[99] and often to many more); the ruin of generals (which recently happened to an exceptional man of the highest capability[100]); and finally the hatred of the common mob, which often results in the expulsion, ruin or flight of men who have rendered great public service. Recall also, on the other side of the coin, the honors, the positions of great power, and the victories. Although these are dependent on Fortune, nevertheless they cannot be carried out—whether the end result is good or bad--without the labors and devotions of men.

It was necessary for us to explain how we can excite and attract the devotions of men for the fulfillment of our purposes. And if this discussion has been rather long, let it be compared with the seriousness of the advantage to be gained. From this perspective, perhaps, it may be seen to be too short.

[21] Whenever men bestow gifts on their fellow men and augment their value or social worth, it may be traced to some reason. One possibility is that it may come from gratitude, when for some reason they have a special regard for someone. Another is that it may come from respect, when they look up to his virtue and believe he is worthy of the best fortune. A third possibility is that they may have faith in him, and believe his actions to be aligned with their own purposes. A fourth possibility is that they

---

[99] The three armies referred to here are the defeat of Pompey at Pharsalus in 48 B.C.; the defeat of Pompey's son at Munda in Spain in 45 B.C.; and the defeat of Metellus Scipio in 46 B.C. at Thapsus in Africa. Julius Caesar routed all of them.

[100] Probably referring to Pompey.

fear his power. A fifth is the opposite possibility: they might expect something from the man of power, as when kings and politicians distribute benefits to people. As a final possibility, they may simply be driven by the desire for money or profit. This last reason is the meanest and basest of all of them, both for those who hold such motives and for those who try to make use of them.

[22] It is a bad situation when something which ought to be done for virtue's sake is instead initiated by the expectation of money. But since this kind of assistance is sometimes necessary, we will discuss how it may be made use of. Before getting into those matters, we will deal with some points related to virtue.

Men place themselves under the authority and power of another for various reasons. They are led on: (a) by goodwill; (b) by the magnitude of the benefits they expect to get; (c) by the other person's high status and the hope that this will be of use to them; (d) by fear that they may be forced to yield to someone else; (e) by an obsession with the hope of receiving bribes or promises of such; and finally, as we have often seen in our own republic, (f) by actually having received money.

VII. [23] Of all possible things, nothing is more felicitous in gaining and safeguarding the hopes of men than to be held in high esteem, and nothing is more alienating to those hopes than to be feared.[101] Ennius said it well with these lines:

> What they fear, they hate. A man hates another, and wishes him to perish.[102]

No amount of resources can withstand the hatred of the majority. If this was not previously known, it certainly has been

---

[101] An interesting (and wiser) counterpoint to Machiavelli's dictum that it is better to be feared than loved.

[102] Apparently a line from Ennius's *Thyestes*.

learned recently. The career of this tyrant,[103] which the state tolerated and obeyed under the weight of arms (even though his death occurred), shows us the extent to which popular hatred can act as a curse. Similar conclusions can be drawn from the fates of other such tyrants, hardly any of which have escaped such a fate. Fear is a poor sentry of long reliability; but devoted goodwill, on the other hand, can stand guard in perpetuity.

[24] But for those rulers who command their populations with an iron fist, cruelty must certainly be used, just as one might do against a domestic servant, if no other means is available. Yet nothing is more insane than the actions of those who, in a free society, create conditions such that they must be feared. Whenever the laws have been submerged under the force of some unjust chicanery, and whenever liberty hides her face in fear, inevitably at some point silent courts emerge, or secret voting on some public office takes place.

Restored liberty bites more fiercely than liberty continuously retained.[104] We must therefore adopt that most widely-appreciated policy (not only for safety's sake but also for the value it brings to the wealth and opportunities of the many) that we banish fear, and hold tightly to mutual affection. Thus may those things we want in both public and private life be more easily pursued. As a matter of fact, those rulers who wish to be feared must necessarily fear those same people whom they seek to rule.

[25] What should we think of the elder Dionysius, who was used to being weighed down by a cross of fear and, fearing the barber's shears, singed off his hair with a red-hot coal?[105] In what

---

[103] The reference is to Julius Caesar.

[104] I.e., when liberty is lost and then won back again, it comes back with a great vengeance.

[105] Repeating a legend about Dionysius, who ruled as tyrant of Syracuse from 406 to 367 B.C.

state of mind do we think Alexander of Pherae lived?[106] We read that he was completely devoted to his wife Thebe, and yet when he went to see her in her room after having finished a meal, he would order one of his barbarian attendants (tattooed like a Thracian) to enter first with a drawn sword to rifle through her jewelry box to see if she had secreted a weapon in her personal effects. What a miserable man is he who would think that a barbarian, a branded slave, would be more faithful than his own wife! And yet he was not so deluded: for he was in fact slain by his own wife, who suspected him of keeping a concubine. No power of authority is so great that it can last for long using the weight of fear.

[26] Consider also Phalaris,[107] who was known more than any other for his cruelty. He was not murdered by treachery, as was Alexander as I described above, and not by a small group, as was our own recent dictator,[108] but rather when the entire population of Agrigentum attacked him. And what else? Did not the Macedonians desert Demetrius and go over *en masse* to Pyrrhus?[109] Do we need another example? Did not nearly all the allies of the Spartans, who were ruling unjustly, abandon them, and sit by passively as they went down in defeat at Leuctra?[110]

---

[106] Tyrant of Pherae in Thessaly in the 4th century B.C. He married the daughter (Thebe) of his predecessor Jason. She had her three brothers assassinate Alexander, allegedly (according to Plutarch) because of her fear of his cruelty.

[107] Phalaris was the tyrant of Agrigentum in Sicily. He was said to have had a bronze bull made for the purpose of roasting alive condemned criminals.

[108] Another reference to Julius Caesar.

[109] Demetrius Poliorcetes, who became ruler of Macedonia in 294 B.C. He alienated his people by his lavish expenditures and arrogant bearing. When Pyrrhus invaded his country in 287, Demetrius's army deserted him and joined Pyrrhus.

[110] At the Battle of Leuctra in 371 B.C., the Spartans were crushed by Thebes and never fully recovered.

VIII. When it comes to illustrating these points, I more easily recall foreign examples than domestic ones. Certainly, however, as long as the empire of the Roman people was held together by a sense of duty, and not by acts of injustice, wars were waged either for the sake of our allies or to maintain our rightful position.

The end of wars usually featured acts of clemency, or other rehabilitative necessities; and the Roman senate was the haven and refuge of kings, nations, and social classes. Our civil office-holders and generals strove to receive the highest praise for this one thing: that they defend our provinces and our allies with equity and fidelity. Thus our system could more accurately be called a "trusteeship of the world" than an empire.

[27] We were gradually over time diminishing this past custom and usage; but after the advent of Sulla we lost it completely.[111] It was not possible to be overly concerned with iniquities against a Roman ally when Roman citizens themselves were being subjected to such cruelty. With regard to Sulla, an honest victory did not proceed from an honest cause. Indeed, when he sold off the possessions of good men and Roman citizens of high distinction, he was insolent enough to say, after having planted a spear in that ground, that he was auctioning off wartime plunder.[112] Sulla was followed by another man engaged in an evil cause; and through the use of an even more foul victory, sold off

---

[111] Cicero is referring to traditional republican practices. The dictator Sulla (138--78 B.C.) was responsible for executing a large number of citizen "enemies of the state" after he assumed full dictatorial power in 81 B.C.

[112] Sulla "proscribed" (i.e., condemned to death without trial) large numbers of political enemies, both real and imagined. Their property was then forfeited to the state and sold off. The traditional symbol of a Roman auction was a spear planted in the ground. This association of a spear with an auction dates to the days when auctions were used as ways of selling off wartime plunder. Cicero, of course, is disgusted with Sulla's pretense in this regard.

the goods not of individual citizens, but gripped entire provinces and regions firmly under one regime of calamity.[113]

[28] So, with foreign nations having been harassed and destroyed, we saw a model of the city of Marseille carried in a triumphal procession as a symbol of lost power.[114] It was celebrated over a city without which none of our generals would have enjoyed a triumph in their wars beyond the Transalpine region. I might, in addition, point out many other nefarious things done against our allies, if the sun had ever seen anything as shameful as this incident. We are punished, therefore, by right. If we had not tolerated the unpunished crimes of so many, never would such license have come to one man. His bequest transmitted his personal effects to a few, but his lust for power infected many unscrupulous men.

[29] The seed and origin of civil wars will never be lacking, so long as corrupt men remember and long for this bloody spear. Publius Sulla rattled that spear while his relative was dictator, and he did not pass up the chance to wave another blood-stained spear thirty-six years later.[115] Another man, who had been a scribe during the first dictatorship, was in the later one a quaestor. From this it ought to be understood that, with such large rewards being available, civil wars will never stop.

For now the walls of our homes stand and endure, but even they stand in fear of external crimes. We have fundamentally lost

---

[113] Another apparent reference to Caesar.

[114] Marseille (Massilia) was a city that had been a traditional ally of Rome. It tried to stay neutral during the civil war between Caesar and Pompey. It refused Caesar admittance in 49 B.C., but did later permit one of Pompey's generals (Lucius Domitius) to enter and command the city. Caesar thus had his justification for besieging and capturing it.

[115] Publius Cornelius Sulla was nephew of the dictator Sulla. Serving as consul in 66 B.C., he was indicted and convicted of bribery. He also gave his uncle the estate of a proscribed man. Later, during the civil war, he was a partisan of Caesar.

the republic. And to return to my original proposition: we came up on this great disaster while we preferred to be feared, rather than to be loved or cared for. If such things could happen to the Roman people collectively, wielding power unjustly, what should *one man* expect? Since it is clear that the power of goodwill is so great, and that of fear is so ineffective, it follows that we should discuss by what methods we may most easily secure, with honor and trust, the affection which we desire.

[30] But we do not all need this to the same extent. Each person's situation in life must be accommodated to its particular extent; that is, whether one needs the affection of many, or whether it is enough to be held in esteem by a few. One thing is certain, though: the first and greatest necessity is to have the loyalty of friends who are devoted to us, and who look up to us. Regarding this fact, there is not much difference between great men and average men. And each one in this respect must be adequately provided for.

[31] Perhaps not all people are equally in need of the glory, endearment, and honor of others. Nevertheless, if these things are at hand, they certainly help a man in many ways, such as in forming friendships.

IX. The subject of friendship was dealt with in anther of my books, entitled *Laelius*.[116] At present let us discuss the topic of Glory, even though two previous books have treated this subject already.[117] Let us examine it here, since it helps a great deal in the handling of a large number of issues.

The purest and most perfect glory is based on three conditions: (1) if the public has special regard for someone; (2) if the public has trust in him; and (3) if the public believes him worthy of the

---

[116] More commonly known as *De amicitia*.

[117] Cicero's lost work *De gloria*. It may have been extant through the Middle Ages, but somehow became finally lost during the Renaissance. Petrarch claimed to have seen it.

honor of admiration. This kind of emotion, if we may state the point simply and briefly, is brought out in individuals in basically the same way as it is from the public at large. But there exists a certain other gateway to the multitude, which permits us to flow, as it were, into the hearts of the many.

[32] With regard to the first of these three conditions I have mentioned above, let us examine the lessons of goodwill. Goodwill is best earned by the performance of regular duties. Secondly, it is also cultivated by the voluntary performance of charitable acts, even though such acts are not required. The public's love is strongly aroused by a man's reputation and fame for liberality, beneficence, justice and fidelity to all of those qualities that relate to mildness and levity of manner.

Since the very quality that we call moral goodness and decorum (because it pleases us by itself and excites our souls by its inner nature and outward aspect) shines through radiantly from those virtues I have noted above, we are forced by Nature herself, therefore, to love those whom we believe possess such virtues. These, indeed, are the most telling causes of devotion; but there may in fact be other less important causes.

[33] Loyalty may be secured with the use of two conditions: (1) if we are considered worldly-wise, and (2) if we have a respectable sense of justice. We have trust in those whom we believe understand more than we, and who can better see the future course of events. When something happens and a crisis hits, we trust him who is able to take action or form a plan at the time. Men consider this type of quality to be valuable and prudent. Trust adheres to men of justice and fidelity—that is, to good men--in a way that they are above any suspicion of deceit or malfeasance. Therefore, we most properly accept the idea of putting our trust in such men for our health, our fortunes and our children.

[34] As far as these two conditions are concerned, justice exerts more influence in promoting confidence, since justice has some authority even without prudence. But prudence without

justice is worth nothing when it comes to instilling confidence. He who is stripped of his reputation for honesty becomes more devious and crafty, and finally, more despised and mistrusted. For this reason, justice welded to intelligence will be the prime mover in securing men's trust, as much as one desires. Justice without good sense can do much; but without justice, good sense will be of little worth.

X. [35] Since it is agreed by all the major philosophers—and it has often been argued by myself also—that he who possesses one virtue has them all, it may be asked why I now separate them. How is it possible for someone who is not prudent to be just? The answer is this: the texture of speech used when "truth" is shaped in educated intellectual debate has one flavor, and that used in the discourse of the common man has quite another. For this reason, then, we speak here as a common man when we say that some men are courageous, some men are good men, and other men are sensible. Colloquial and commonly-known words must be used when we speak on topics of popular concern, in the same way that Panaetius did.

But let us return to our original question.

[36] The third condition (of the three listed above relating to glory) is that we be judged worthy of the admiration and respect of other men. All people commonly admire those things that are great, or which they notice as exceeding their preconceptions; and with regard to individuals, they admire those good qualities that they had not thought were present. They look up to those men, and lavish the greatest praise on those whom they believe to possess singular and unusual virtues; but they despise and look down on those whom they think have no character, no spirit or no resolution.

Not everyone condemns those whom they believe to be bad. They do not condemn those whom they believe to be morally unsound, abusive, deceitful or plotters of mischief; but they certainly believe such men to be wicked. For this reason, as I said before, they condemn those who are "worthless to themselves and to others," as the saying goes. That is, they condemn those who have no work ethic, no industry and no thought of the future.

[37] Those who inspire admiration are those who are thought to exceed others in virtue and are lacking in all types of misbehavior as well as those vices that others cannot easily resist. Physical pleasure, that most addictive of mistresses, deflects the souls of the majority of men from the path of virtue; and, when the firebrands of sorrow draw near, most of such men are quite paralyzed with terror.[118]

Life, death, riches and poverty: all of these things agitate men most intensely. When those who adopt a lofty and exalted spirit express contempt for their present situation (however good or bad it may be), and when some noble opportunity presents itself to them, seizes them wholly and converts them to its virtuous purpose, who then cannot be in awe at the magnificence and surpassing beauty of virtue?

XI. [38] Just as this elevation of mind promotes great admiration in others, so to a great extent justice, the one virtue on which men are judged to be truly good, is seen by the public as being truly magical. And the public is perfectly justified in this. No one can be truly just who fears death, suffering, exile and material loss. Nor can anyone be just who places the opposites of these things ahead of equity. People greatly admire the man who is unmoved by money. If such a man is encountered by the public, they think him tested by fire.

Therefore, these three conditions which have been proposed as sources of glory are all realized through justice: *goodwill* wants to be useful to the most people; likewise *trust*, for the same reason; and lastly *admiration*, because it spurns and rejects these things, with which many are possessed by a burning avidity.

---

[118] The reference to the "firebrands of sorrow" may subtly suggest the burning sensation of a sexually transmitted disease.

[39] By my way of thinking, every rule and institution of life requires the assistance of other men; most importantly, so that a man might have fellows with whom to interact socially. Unless you carry the countenance of a good man, this can be difficult. Thus, even for a solitary man living in the countryside, it is necessary to have a reputation for justice. Perhaps even more so: because if they do not have this good reputation, but rather are seen as unjust, they are not protected by any defenses and so may be afflicted by many injuries from others.

[40] So also with regard to those who sell, buy, enter into contracts, utilize agreements and are involved in commercial dealings, justice is necessary for conducting business. Its power is such that not even those who live off deception and crime can long survive without some measure of justice. If we imagine one of these types—a robber, for example—who snatches or steals something as a "captain" of a robber crew, we can see that he would lose his place in the gang if he did not divide up the plunder equally among the other members. They would either kill such a ringleader or abandon him.

Indeed, there are said to exist rules among bandits to which they are subject, and which they obey. Because of his equitable division of spoils, Bardulis, the Illyrian robber (whom we find mentioned in Theopompus) amassed certain riches.[119] Viriathus the Lusitanian amassed even greater plunder.[120] Our army and generals were even forced to leave him alone. But the praetor Caius Laelius,[121] who used the surname "Sapiens" (the Wise), smashed this bandit and shattered his power, decisively putting

---

[119] Bardulis was an Illyrian bandit chief who eventually rose to great power in his country. Theopompus (c.380—315 B.C.) was a pupil of Isocrates and a historian who wrote a continuation of the history of Thucydides.
[120] Viriathus was a local leader in Lusitania who led (c.147 B.C.) an armed resistance against the Romans.
[121] Caius Laelius was praetor in 145 B.C.

him in check, to such an extent that he bequeathed an easy mopping-up to those who took office after him.

If the power of justice is so great that it can support and elevate even the fortunes of bandits, how much power do we think it can bring to bear on laws, courts and the constitution of a republic?

XII. [41] It seems to me, in fact, that not only among the Medes (as Herodotus tells us), but also among our own ancestors, kings of good moral character were chosen so that others might be able thereby to enjoy justice.[122] For when the multitude was oppressed by the classes who controlled the wealth, they tried to seek recourse in someone of outstanding virtue, someone who might shield them from abuses; and by establishing equal justice, such a man would hold the highest and lowest sectors of society to a uniform rule of law. The reason for establishing laws and the reason for establishing kingdoms was thus the same.

[42] Law is always sought for the sake of equity. If it were otherwise, there would be no law. When the multitude was following the guidance of one just and good man, they were satisfied with that; but when this option was not available, laws were invented which would speak consistently to both the individual and to the group in one clear voice.

It can be seen from this, then, that in the selection of leaders, it was customary for men to be chosen who had, in the public's opinion, a great reputation for justice. If joined to this such men also possessed prudence, then there was nothing under such leadership that men might think was beyond their capabilities. By every method, then, justice must be cultivated and preserved, not only for its own sake—for otherwise justice does not exist—but also for the sake of raising our own personal honor and glory. Just as there is not only a way to earn money, but also in fact a way to invest it so that it meets our perpetual expenses (not only the

---

[122] *See* Herod. I.96.

necessary expenses, but also the more diversionary ones), so likewise glory must be pursued and "invested" through the use of some method.

[43] Socrates once beautifully said that the shortest road--and short-cut--to glory was this: *if one acts in some way that he wishes to be perceived, then that is the sort of person he will actually be.* Those who think that they can attain glory by deceit, inane ostentation, or by inventing words and facial expressions, are seriously wrong. True glory has roots which are widely spread out; all fake things quickly fall away like little flowers, and nothing false can pass itself off as long-lasting. Many witnesses exist for each side of this question, but for the sake of brevity, we will satisfy ourselves with a look at one family. Tiberius Gracchus, the son of Publius, will be praised for as long as the memory of Roman greatness lasts.[123] But his sons were not sanctioned by good men while they were alive; and in death, they number among those who were deservedly slain.[124]

XIII. He who wishes to pursue true glory, then, should be engaged in the duties of justice. What these are has already been discussed in the preceding book.

[44] So that we may more easily *be seen* to be what we actually *wish* to be—for this is the most important point here—certain rules must be given. In this way we will become those things which we wish to be considered. If someone from an early age has a patrimony by reason of celebrity, family name or father (as I believe is true in your case, my dear Cicero[125]), or by some special circumstance or situation, all the eyes of the world fall on

---

[123] Tiberius Gracchus was tribune in 187 B.C. and later fought a successful war in Spain. As consul in 177 B.C. he subjugated Sardinia. He was also censor in 169 B.C.

[124] This is of course a reference to Tiberius and Caius Gracchus, the sons who tried to be political reformers.

[125] Cicero sometimes refers to his son Marcus as "Cicero."

him. They probe into what he does and how he lives. Just as if he conducts himself in the glare of a spotlight, nothing he says or does can be kept in the dark.

[45] Those youths who, because of their common origins and obscurity, are not widely known to the public from their early years, ought to set their sights high from the time they begin to become young adults, and make moves towards desired goals with intense efforts. They will do this with a robust spirit, for at that age they are not only not begrudged their goals but are actually favored. The first suggestion to a youth seeking glory is that it may be gained through military service. Many of our ancestors gained prominence in this same way, as wars were nearly always being waged.

Your own current age has encountered war, in which one side possesses excessive evil, and the other side too little good fortune. In this present civil war, when Pompey appointed you to command a military unit, extensive praise was given you by that great man and his army for your cavalry skills, use of javelins, and ability to withstand the rigors of military life.[126] Yet your glory, indeed, came to an end, along with the old republic. This discussion was not undertaken to relate your personal fortunes, but rather to deal with glory generally. Let us, then, turn our attention to the remaining topics of discussion.

[46] Just as in most things the more important work is done with the mind than with the body, the things which we seek through reason and our natural disposition are more profitable than those attained through raw strength. The first recommendation for someone seeking glory starts with modesty, with devotion to one's parents, and with kindness towards them.

---

[126] Pompey appointed the young Cicero (then only about seventeen years old) to command a squadron of auxiliary cavalry called an *ala*, which consisted of 300 to 400 men.

However, the young men recognized most easily, and in the best way, are those who associate themselves with prominent and wise men who are also good stewards of their governments. And if they spend enough time with such wise men, they promote the public's confidence that they will emulate these men whom they have selected as mentors.

[47] The home of Publius Mucius was useful to the young Publius Rutilius for acquainting him with the idea of character and a knowledge of law.[127] Lucius Crassus, however, when he was just as much an adolescent, did not borrow his reputation from anyone else. He himself achieved his own praise from that important and incredible indictment.[128] At an age when others engaged in the practice of rhetoric are used to being swayed by praise, Lucius Crassus displayed at this age—just as tradition tells us about Demosthenes—an impressive ability to conduct himself in legal venues. He certainly was able to plan his cases at home to great effect.

XIV. [48] But in speech there are basically two divisions: one is *discourse*, and the other is *active debate*. There really is no doubt that debate has the greater power in achieving glory (this is the eloquence we speak of here). Nevertheless, it is difficult to say to what extent politeness and courtesy in discussion may win the hearts of others. The letters of Philip to Alexander, of Antipater to

---

[127] Publius Mucius Scaevola was consul in 133 B.C. and father of Quintus Mucius Scaevola. He was known for his extensive knowledge of law (the *ius pontificium*). Publius Rutilius Rufus was consul in 105 B.C. and later proconsul in Asia. He was later indicted for malfeasance, but the charges against him appear to have been trumped up by political enemies.

[128] This is a reference to a successful prosecution conducted by the 21-year-old Crassus against a politician named Caius Carbo.

Cassander[129] and of Antigonus to Philip the Younger[130] are still extant; these three personalities, we are assured, are among the most far-sighted in history. They instruct us to win over the minds of men to goodwill by affable speech and to retain the loyalty of soldiers by persuasive appeals.

When a speech is made before a large audience on some litigated matter, it often generates widespread renown. The deliverer receives great admiration for his fluid and wise words; and when the listeners hear him, they believe him to be more intelligent and wise than they. If in his oration the speaker combines modesty with gravitas, then nothing is more admirable. The achievement is even greater if we find such qualities in a young man.

[49] While there are many types of motives for speaking where eloquence is needed, a good number of young men in our republic achieve notoriety in speaking before tribunals, before the people, and before the senate. But the most admiration comes from the speeches before the courts.

With regard to courtroom oratory, there are two divisions. We have the oratory from the prosecution, and that from the defense. Working for the defense is generally more praiseworthy, but quite often the prosecution side should be commended as well. I spoke earlier about the abilities of Crassus; but the young Marcus Antonius did nearly the same thing. An indictment also showed clearly the eloquence of Publius Sulpicius, when he hauled a

---

[129] Antipater (397—319 B.C.) was a Macedonian general who became regent of Alexander the Great's empire in 320 B.C. His son was Cassander (c.350—297 B.C.), who became king of Macedon in 305 B.C.
[130] Antigonus III Doson (263—221 B.C.) administered Macedon as trustee for the young Philip V (c.238—179 B.C.).

corrupt and conspiratorial citizen named Caius Norbanus before a tribunal.[131]

[50] But this must not be done too often. It is only appropriate in matters affecting the welfare of the republic, as in the situations I described above. It may also be merited for the purpose of avenging wrongs (as in the example of the two Luculli), or for the defense of others (as I did for the Sicilians, or as Julius did in Sardinia when he indicted Albucius). The diligence of Lucius Fufius in his prosecution of Manius Aquilius is also a well-known example.[132]

But this sort of event may happen only once in a career, or at least very infrequently. If it happens that such prosecutions must be done more often, let any advocate treat it as a gift to his country. For he must not too often be held back from punishing the enemies of his nation. Nevertheless, even in this there must be some due process. It seems to take a harsh man, or a man bereft of human emotion, to bring to trial a large number of capital cases.[133] It is dangerous for a prosecutor, and damaging to his reputation, to be permanently labeled as a "prosecutor." This label was attached to Marcus Brutus, who came from a very distinguished family; he was also the son of an eminent authority on the civil law.

[51] This principle of duty must be diligently adhered to: never to summon a capital indictment against someone whose guilt is not certain. No such thing can be done without the

---

[131] Caius Norbanus was prosecuted for sedition in 94 B.C. by Publius Sulpicius Rufus. Marcus Antonius defended him successfully.

[132] Aquilius was acquitted in this prosecution, probably because of his earlier service to the state. But his greed eventually caught up with him in 88 B.C. He was captured by Mithridates VI and executed by having molten gold poured down his throat.

[133] This did not necessarily mean a case involving the possible forfeiture of life. It could also mean a case where a person could suffer loss of citizenship.

prosecutor himself becoming a criminal. For what could be more inhuman than to turn the eloquence given by Nature for the safety and protection of mankind, to the cause of ruining and destroying the good? And although this must be avoided, there is no harm done to our obligations if at some time we must plead for the defense, unless the defendant is utterly depraved or evil. The multitude wants this; tradition tolerates it; and human nature makes it happen.

The burden is always on the judge to seek the truth; for the defense advocate, the burden is to adhere close to the truth, even if he may fall somewhat short of that. Frankly, I would not dare make such a statement (especially since I am writing a book on moral philosophy!), if this were not also the position of that most ethical of Stoics, Panaetius. The greatest glory and thanks go to the defense (and even more, if it happens) when those who appear to be beaten down and oppressed by the rich and powerful are rescued. I have done this often, especially in my youth. You may recall I defended Sextus Roscius of Ameria against the power of the despot Lucius Sulla. That speech, as you know, is still extant.[134]

XV. [52] Having dealt with the responsibilities of the young, which are useful in the attainment of glory, the duties of generosity and kindness must now be described. It has two types: works of charity towards the indigent or the offering of money. Money is the easier route, especially for the rich; but personal service is more elegant, more impressive, and more dignified for a strong and high-minded man. Although in each method there exists the impulse to satisfy one's generosity, nevertheless, one method is derived from the money-box and the other from virtue.

---

[134] This speech, *Pro Roscio Amerino*, was delivered by Cicero in 80 B.C. Sextus Roscius was tried for patricide. Cicero's successful defense implicated one of Sulla's cronies, Lucius Cornelius Chrysogonus, a fact which did not endear him to the ruthless Sulla.

The generosity which comes from one's personal savings depletes the fountain of benevolence. Kindness is cancelled with kindness; for the more you use it for the sake of the many, the less you have that can be used.

[53] But if those who are kind and generous instead use their personal qualities and work, we see that (1) when they provide value to many people, they generate more helpers in performing their charitable causes; and (2) they become more practiced in the habits of kindness and, we can say, more skilled at providing charity to many.

King Philip of Macedon, in one letter to his son Alexander, chastised him for attempting to win the good-will of his subjects by bribery. "What poor thinking," he counseled, "made you cling to this hope, that those whom you corrupted with gifts would be loyal to you? Or are you acting this way so that the Macedonians will view you not as their king, but as their servant and quartermaster?"

"Servant and quartermaster" was the appropriate usage here, because it was demeaning for a king to act this way. It was even better when Philip noted that the bribes were "corrupting." For he who accepts bribes begins a slide to ruin: he becomes ever more ready to expect larger gifts.

[54] This advice was for Philip's son, but we can see that the point applies universally. For there is no doubt that this kind of benevolence, which manifests itself in good works and industry, is more honest, extends more widely in scope, and can be of use to more people. Nevertheless, sometimes contributions should be given to those in need, and this type of kindness should not be completely forgotten. Often we should make some provision from our store of funds for those people who are indigent, but do so carefully, and with moderation. Many people have dissipated their inheritances with frivolous largesse. What is more foolish than to do something you enjoy doing in such a way that you eventually prevent yourself from doing it? In addition, plunder seems to

follow from excessive generosity. When too much charity begins to cause cravings from need, some will feel compelled to lay their hands on the possessions of other men. When people want to be generous for the purpose of cultivating favor, the devotion that is aroused in those to whom they give gifts is not as great as the resentment generated in those from whom they confiscate wealth.

[55] For this reason, we should neither shut our wallets too tightly, so that we never open them for charity, nor carelessly flaunt them openly to the world. The way we deploy our resources should be matched to our means. We ought well to remember that old saying which through common use has become something of a proverb for our people: "Lavish giving has no bottom."[135] Indeed how could there be any limits, when those who are used to getting gifts want to continue getting them, and those who do not have them, want them?

XVI. There are basically two categories of large donors. One is excessive, and the other is more governed by a spirit of tasteful liberality. The wasteful spenders are those who dole out their money in banquets, feasts, gladiatorial combats, public games and animal fights. Only a faint memory, or none at all, of these things will have been left once they are finished. The more restrained type of benefactor, however, is the kind of man who uses his own resources to ransom captives from pirates, or helps his friends by assuming their debts or providing for their daughters' dowries, or otherwise helping them with what they need, or increasing what they have.

[56] For this reason, I am a bit bewildered as to what Theophrastus had in mind when he wrote his book *On Riches*. There are many good things to be found in this treatise, but I found

---

[135] The actual saying is *largitionem fundum non habere*. *Fundum* can also mean *foundation*, but the context here clearly implicates the idea of limits, which makes the better rendering "bottom."

this to be absurd: he thinks that the splendor of giving lavish public spectacles should be much praised, and that this is the best way to find profit in one's riches. For me, however, the real benefit of generosity is to be found in the examples previously given above. They are significantly larger and more reliable.

How much more well-grounded and true is Aristotle on this matter, when he scolds us for not being shocked at the squandering of money which is done to appease the ignorant mob. He tells us that:

> If people during a military siege are forced to pay a mina for a *sextarius* of water, this at first appears to us incredible, and everyone is shocked.[136] But then when they reflect on it, they make allowances for the extreme hardship at issue. In other sorts of gross wastage and conspicuous consumption, though, we are not so stricken with wonder: not even when no dire need is involved and no sort of dignity is promoted. The enjoyment of the crowd is engaged only for a short, fleeting time. And this itself is the most trifling thing of all: as soon as the senses of the person are satisfied, the memory of the event dies away.[137]

[57] He then quite rightly concludes: "This sort of thing may be gratifying to children, women, slaves and those who are like slaves; but they can in no way be endorsed by a serious man and by those who concern themselves with what is right." I understand, of course, that formerly in our own country during good times, such displays were publicly offered by the best men during their tenure in office as aediles. Thus Publius Crassus, who had the cognomen of "The Rich," put on many lavish games

---

[136] A *sextarius* was a Roman unit of liquid measure, equal to one sixth of a *congius*. Its closest modern equivalent would be about a pint or one-half liter.
[137] This quote and the one that follows must be from a lost treatise of Aristotle. They are not found in any currently known text.

during his aedileship. A little time after this Lucius Crassus, with that most moderate of men Quintus Mucius, did the same. Finally, Caius Claudius (the son of Appius) offered his own games, followed by the Luculli, Hortensius and Silanus. Better than all of these was Publius Lentulus during the time I won the consulship. And then Lentulus was imitated by Scaurus. During his second consulship our own Pompey exceeded all who came before him. From all this I think you can get an idea of my thoughts about lavish entertainments.

XVII. [58] By the same token, one must take care not to surround oneself with the aura of miserliness. Mamercus, an extremely rich man, brought defeat on himself in the race for the consulship, after he had passed over the aedileship.[138] Clearly, if such public entertainments are desired by the people, they should be provided by the astute leader, even if he privately dislikes such spectacles. But he should keep them within reason, as I myself did as consul, if at some time something greater and more useful is acquired from the people by bribery. The public feasts given in the streets by Orestes (which he called a "tithe offering") are an example; these brought him much favor.

No one thought it was a problem when Marcus Seius capped the sale of corn at one *as* per *modium* as a charitable measure.[139] He was thus able to remove the longstanding, acrimonious, and seething antagonism of the people against him, in a most efficient way. But the highest of our honors goes to Milo who, having purchased some gladiators for public entertainment (for which I bore the expense of maintenance), then crushed all the plans and

---

[138] Mamercus Aemilius Lepidus Livianus was consul in 77 B.C.

[139] An *as* is a Roman copper monetary unit, and a *modium* is a unit of measure, equal to about one peck (or 8.8 liters). Marcus Seius was quaestor in 80 B.C. and aedile in 74 B.C.

ludicrous schemes of Publius Clodius.[140]

[59] Lavish giving, therefore, should have a justification based on either necessity or practical advantage. And when it has to be done, the rule of moderation is the best guideline. Indeed, Lucius Philippus, the son of Quintus, a man of great character and noted distinction, was in the habit of boasting that he had won all the most important offices of the state without having to render gifts to anyone. Cotta and Curio used to say the same thing.[141] In some ways, I could pride myself on this point also. For I rose through elected offices of the republic (to which I was unanimously elected as soon as I was eligible, something that none of the men just mentioned were able to do), with only a small expense to my aedileship.[142]

[60] This sort of spending is much more agreeable when used for walls, shipping docks, ports, aqueducts and all those things connected to state use. Of course, something that is doled out into a person's hand is more delightful; but posterity will be more grateful for the things just mentioned. I abstain slightly from criticizing the construction of theaters, colonnades and new temples, out of respect for Pompey. But the most learned men do not really recommend them. Panaetius is one of these, and in these books I am striving to practice his teachings, not merely to paraphrase them.

So also did Demetrius of Phalerum scold Pericles, the most

---

[140] Titus Annius Milo was a friend of Cicero and had tried to have him brought back from exile. He was prosecuted for the murder of Clodius in 52 B.C. and was unsuccessfully defended by Cicero (see Cicero's speech *Pro Milone*). It was also Clodius who had been responsible for Cicero's exile.

[141] The reference is to Caius Aurelius Cotta (consul in 75 B.C.) and Caius Scribonius Curio (consul in 76 B.C.).

[142] Cicero rose through the *cursus honorum* rapidly. He was elected quaestor at age 31; aedile at 37; praetor at 40; and finally consul at 43. For someone not from a patrician family, this was an impressive achievement.

prominent Greek leader, when he funneled so much money into the brilliant Propylaea.[143] But this entire subject was dealt with extensively in my work *De re publica*. We may conclude, finally, that all of these types of lavish giving fall into the category of vice: they must be accommodated only according to one's financial abilities, and controlled by adhering to the principle of moderation.

XVIII. [61] In the other type of money-giving (that is, the type of which comes from tasteful liberality) we should not be inclined to one way of thinking when considering different circumstances. One situation is that of a man who is hard-pressed by some calamity. Another case is that of the man who, even though he is not facing any adversity, seeks to improve his condition.

[62] Charity ought to be more inclined to cases of severe calamity, unless those hit by calamity were deserving of it. And with regard to those who wish to be helped so that they are not completely destroyed, but rather wish to rise up to a better condition, we ought to be in no way stingy in our efforts to aid them. But in selecting such people for assistance, we ought to be guided by good sense and moderation. Ennius made this point amusingly:

I see good deeds wrongly placed as bad deeds indeed.

[63] A good and grateful man delights in the appreciation bestowed on him from this sort of act and by the favor given to him from others. When rashness is absent, generosity is most acceptable and is most eagerly praised by the majority, because the benevolence of influential people is everyone's common refuge. Efforts, therefore, must be made to influence as many

---

[143] This was an expensive and impressive structure located at the entrance of the Acropolis at Athens.

people as possible with such charitable gifts, so that they are remembered by the children and descendants of the original recipients. In this way, they all cannot help but be grateful. Every person hates ingratitude when it comes to charity, and sees it as a vice against himself, since it tends to deter generosity. They see the ingrate as the common enemy of all those who are without resources.

These types of kindnesses are useful for a republic: the recovery of enslaved prisoners of war and the alleviating of the misery of the poor. This policy is also a good one for non-state actors; and we see much written in an oration of Crassus that this kind of generosity was a policy in our order.[144] I much more favor this type of charity than the lavish doling out of money. It is a type of charity suited for serious and great men, while the other type is more suited for the lackeys of the common mob, that is, those who like to titillate people's shallowness with empty pleasures.

[64] It is appropriate to be generous in giving and at the same time not overbearing in carrying out agreements already entered into, whether they be for buying and selling, bringing together contracts or farming them out, or whether we are dealing with acquaintances or familial relations. One should also be just and courteous, and willing to cede much of one's legal rights if need be, and to shun lawsuits as much as may be permitted (and perhaps a little more). Not only is it sometimes honorable to relinquish one's legal rights, but it is also sometimes profitable. We must exercise prudence when it comes to our personal property, for it is a disgrace to allow it to dissipate carelessly. But this should be done in such a way that we are beyond suspicion of miserliness and greed. The ability to make use of generosity in a way that we do not plunder our inheritance is without doubt the greatest enjoyment of money.

Hospitality is rightly praised by Theophrastus. It seems to me,

---

[144] I.e., in the order of knights, or *equites*.

at least, that the homes of distinguished men should be open to visits by illustrious guests. It is also a noteworthy feature of our own republic that foreign visitors do not lack for this sort of accommodation here in our city. It is also exceedingly useful to those who honorably wish to be able to gain favor with their guests by using resources and gratitude, and thereby win influence among foreign peoples. Indeed, Theophrastus wrote that Cimon of Athens had been hospitable to the Laciads, who were part of his political subdivision.[145] He supervised this himself, and ordered his subordinates to make all necessary accommodations whenever a Laciad might see him at his villa.

XIX. [65] Those services that are not given as monetary gifts of generosity may be conferred on the state and on individual citizens. To render legal aid, to offer effective counsel and to be of use to as many as possible in this regard, are all directly related to the augmenting of one's influence and popularity. Among the many great traditions of our ancestors, one of the best was the study and interpretation of the civil law, for which they always had the highest regard. Indeed, before our own present age of turbulence, the leading men of government held firmly to this knowledge. But now the splendor of this legal wisdom and the public offices commanding dignity have been blotted out. This situation is all the more unjust because it has developed during the lifetime of a man who was equal to all who came before him in honor and who in knowledge easily outdistances them.[146]

All these types of works are agreeable to many, and are well-adapted to the binding of men together through reciprocal benefits.

---

[145] The word used here is *curiales*, which is the name given to leading members of large clan. But the context suggests more of a political unit.
[146] This is a reference to Cicero's friend Servius Sulpicius Rufus (106-43 B.C.), a distinguished jurist and rhetor.

[66] Public speaking is a companion art to the legal profession. As a skill it is more agreeable, serious and worthy of respect. For what can take the place of eloquence in arousing the admiration of listeners, the hopes of the needy or the thanks of the accused defendant? It was for this skill that our ancestors awarded the foremost "toga of honor."[147] Substantial benefits and the ability to help others are available to hard-working men of eloquence who adopt the ways of our forefathers by defending many cases willingly and without expectation of pay.

[67] Something cautions me, at this point, to take note of the current lack of eloquence, or rather its complete ruin, even though I fear I may be seen as complaining for my own self-serving reasons. But we see how many orators have been destroyed; we see the scant hope there is in the remaining few, and the lack of competence that they have, as well as their arrogance. Although not everyone (very few in fact) can be skilled or erudite in the practice of law, one may nevertheless be of use to many by reaching out to do good works, by testifying before jurors and magistrates, by being vigilant for one another's interests, and by taking care of those whom one advises or defends. Those who do these things receive the greatest amount of thanks and their diligent activity carries over into many other fields.

[68] Since it is an obvious thing, people in this position do not need to be reminded to pay attention that when they give help to some they do not offend others. For often they hurt those whom they should not, and offend those whom it is very unwise to offend. If they are unintentional in such acts, then it is simple negligence; but if they know what they are doing, it is pure rashness. Such a person must, as much as possible, offer an apology to those whom he might have accidentally hurt. He should also explain why it happened, why it was done out of

---

[147] I.e., a symbol of the highest virtue.

144

necessity and could not have happened differently and how he plans to compensate the person who may have been violated through works of restitution or other services.

XX. [69] When helping other people, a person generally examines the circumstances beyond their control and their behavior. It is easy to say—and therefore commonly repeated— that when it comes to granting benefits on others, one should look at the behavior of the grantees rather than at the circumstances beyond their control. This is a worthy statement. But who when performing a service places the favor of the most deserving but poor man ahead of the interests of a fortunate and rich man? Our propensity is generally to favor him from whom we believe remuneration will arrive with more speed and less trouble.

But we must take note more carefully of how things really are. Without doubt a poor man, if he is a good man, will certainly be grateful even if he is unable to return the favor. Someone made this point most suitably when he said: "He who may have money, has not repaid it; who has repaid it, does not have it. Who returns a favor, however, still has it; and he who may still have it, has repaid it."[148] But those who believe themselves to be rich, special, or better than others, definitely do not want to be obligated to others' kindnesses. Such people actually believe they *have given a benefit* to the donor when they accept some large gift. They also assume something substantial is then expected from them in return, or will be demanded from them. They believe that making use of a patron or being called a client is a fate worse than death.

[70] The impoverished man believes that whatever is done for him is done for his personal betterment rather than out of pity for the condition Fortune has put him in. He is eager to seem grateful

---

[148] The pun in the Latin (playing on the idea of "having" something) is lost in English, but the idea is that even after someone "pays back" a favor, he will still be grateful for the favor that was originally done for him.

not only to him who has already helped him, but also to those from whom he expects help later. For he certainly needs help from many. He also does not hyperbolize the service he does out of thanks in return (if he renders any in reciprocation) with words of puffery; instead, he downplays his work.

And there is something else that must be appreciated here also. If you defend a rich person favored by Fortune, gratitude will come from him only, and (if you are lucky) his children. But if you defend a poor man who is good and honest, the rest of the good and honest poor people (of which there are a great number) will see that a bulwark of justice has been raised for them. It is for this reason that I believe it is better to render benefits to the good than to those lucky ones blessed by Fortune.

[71] We must exert all possible efforts in order to assist all types of men adequately. But if some conflict of interest arises in this effort, we should without doubt look to Themistocles as an authority. When he was asked, on the subject of his daughter's hand in marriage, whether he would prefer a poor but good man to a rich but unreliable man, he said: "Truly, I prefer a man who is lacking in money, than money which is lacking in a man." Yet morals have been corrupted and perverted by our admiration of riches.

Why should the size of someone else's riches matter at all to one of us? Wealth perhaps helps the man who has it, but not always. Imagine that it does help someone. He certainly may have more money to spend, but how does this make him a better man? And if he happens to be a rich man, let not his riches be an impediment to your helping him; but also do not let his wealth be the reason for your giving help. The decision to render aid to a man should be based entirely on his character, not on his riches.

The final rule in conferring benefits and works is this: you should never contend against what is fair and equitable, and never advocate for what is wrong. For justice is the foundation of lasting commendation and fame, and nothing can be praiseworthy without justice.

XXI. [72] Because we have now treated those types of benefits which relate to individuals, we must now discuss those which relate to groups and to a civil state. Of these, there are some that pertain to all citizens and some that adhere only to individuals. The benefits adhering to individuals produce more in the way of thanks. If possible, we should perform service for each category. And when we are providing benefits to individuals, we must do so in such a way that the benefit advances (or at least does not hurt) the interests of the state.

For example, Caius Gracchus established huge public donations of grain; but this practice exhausted the treasury. The system of Marcus Octavius, in contrast, was tolerable for the state and essential for the lower classes; we can thus say it was a healthy measure for both citizens and state.[149]

[73] It must be seen as among the first duties of any man who helps administer a republic to ensure that each man is secure in his own property and that he is not faced with the threat of confiscation of his private goods. Philippus, when he was tribune, disastrously brought out his agrarian law; and when this law easily suffered defeat, he showed himself very much to be restrained in his reaction.[150] But when he used to address the crowds he adopted a vehement tone designed to win public support. "There are not two thousand people in the state," he said, "who own property." This is dangerous talk and directly implicates the equal redistribution of property. What curse could be worse than this? Republics and states have been constituted specifically for the purpose of ensuring that each person may keep his own property.

---

[149] Gracchus's law provided for a monthly ration of grain (five *modii*) for each citizen at rates far below market prices. Octavius as tribune in 120 B.C. passed a law that raised grain prices.

[150] It is not clear what law is being referred to here, but the point is to accuse him of demagoguery.

Although men began to congregate into communities under the influence of Nature, they still sought the protection of cities under the hope that they might safeguard their possessions.

[74] It used to happen that a certain type of tax was levied on our ancestors, since in those days the treasury was often in a precarious state and wars were frequent.[151] But now all care must be taken that this be avoided, and this care must be applied well in advance to make sure such a tax is unnecessary. But if dire necessity imposes such a duty on any state, all steps must be taken to let the population know that, if they wish to be saved from such a crisis, they must yield to extraordinary measures. (I am not talking about our own state. Rather than presage hypothetical events about our country, I prefer to speak of "states" in a general sense). Furthermore, all those who rule the state ought to take scrupulous care that an adequate reserve of life-sustaining provisions has been stockpiled. It is not necessary to get into the specifics of how this normally happens, or ought to happen, for the matter is an obvious one. The topic need only be mentioned.

[75] The most vital thing in any responsibility of office or charge of duty is that the slightest hint of corruption should be avoided. "I only wish," said Caius Pontius the Samnite, "that Fortune had spared me from living in this era, and instead I had been born at a time when the Romans began to accept bribes! I would not have to tolerate their rule over us much longer."[152] He would not have had to wait for many centuries, for this evil has invaded our republic only recently.

I can happily deal with the fact that Pontius was born a long

---

[151] There was a provision for levying a property tax (*tributum*) in the old republic to raise revenues for war. This was gradually phased out, however, after the conquest of Macedonia.

[152] Caius Pontius was a Samnite general who defeated the Romans in 321 B.C. at the Caudine Forks.

time ago, as he was a man stronger than oak. It is not yet even a hundred and ten years since the law of Lucius Piso was enacted for the recovery of extorted money.[153] There had not been anything similar before this law. But since that time, we saw so many laws, each one more vigorous than its predecessor. We saw how many were convicted, and how many sentenced. We saw how such a "social war" was stirred up out of fear of what our courts might do. And when the laws were repealed and the courts relented, we saw how awful was the looting and ransacking of the allies. The end result is that we are strong now not so much through our own merit but because of the feebleness of all the others.[154]

XXII. [76] Panaetius praises Africanus for his restraint.[155] And why would he not applaud him? Yet he had something greater. Africanus's merit did not just come from him personally, but also from the times he lived in. All the treasure of the Macedonians, which was huge, Paulus acquired and added to the Roman treasury; and this massive requisition from a single general brought an end to the need for tax levies on Roman citizens.[156] Yet Paulus brought none of this into his own house, save for the eternal memory of his name. Africanus followed his father's example, and was no richer after he completed the destruction of Carthage. Consider also Lucius Mummius, his colleague in the censorship. Did Mummius come out any richer,

---

[153] The *res repetundae* called for the restoration of extorted monies by corrupt officials. Lucius Calpurnius Piso Frugi was consul in 133 B.C.

[154] Cicero here is referring to the so-called "Social War" (90--88 B.C.), in which the Romans fought a revolt of some city-states (*socii*, or "allies") of the Italic peninsula.

[155] Scipio Aemilianus, also known as Scipio Africanus the Younger (185—129 B.C.).

[156] So much money came into the treasury from the conquest of Macedonia that the *tributum* property tax became unnecessary. See section [74] above.

after he had completely overthrown the most opulent of all cities?[157] He preferred to adorn Italy than his own house; and yet it seems to me that, with Italy adorned, his own house became so much more brilliant.

[77] To return to the subject from which we have briefly digressed: no vice is more disgraceful than greed, especially when it is found in the ruling elites of a nation. To extract profit from one's position of leadership is not only morally reprehensible, but criminal and evil. So when the Pythian Apollo prophesized that Sparta would only be destroyed through greed, it seems to me that the oracle predicted the fate not only of the Spartans, but also that of other wealthy nations. In no other way can those who are in charge of the state more easily win over the goodwill of the multitude than by exercising self-control and continence.

[78] Both those who pander to the masses and propose agrarian "reform" with demagogic motivations, so that the rightful possessors of land are driven off, and those who wish to see debtors' obligations to creditors forgiven, undermine the foundations of the state. They destroy harmony, in the first place, which cannot exist when monies are confiscated from some and then given to others; secondly, they destroy the concept of fairness, which is taken away for everyone when a person cannot retain what is rightfully his. A special characteristic of the city and the civil state, as I said earlier, is the right of secure and undisturbed control of one's own possessions.

[79] And in this ruin of a republic which follows from such policies, the demagogues do not even get the adulation they seek. For he who has had something taken from him is now an enemy; and he who has been given something conceals the fact that he wanted to receive it. To a great extent he hides his joy in the

---

[157] The general Lucius Mummius Achaicus sacked the wealthy Greek city of Corinth in 146 B.C on orders from the Roman senate.

discharge of his debts out of fear that he might be seen as having been financially distressed. But without doubt, the person who has suffered the dispossession remembers it and carries his grief around with him.

Even if there are more people who have been wrongfully given property than there are those from whom property has been confiscated, it does not follow that the former wield more political influence. These types of issues are decided not by number, but by weight. How can there be any justice when a man who had nothing suddenly has lands that were owned by another for years or even generations? And where is the justice when the man who previously owned land has suddenly lost it?

XXIII. [80] It was because of this same kind of evil that the Lacedaemonians expelled the ephor[158] Lysander and executed King Agis, something that had never happened before in that state. As a result, from this time forward, such terrible discord followed that tyrants appeared on the scene, the leading societal figures were banished and a brilliantly constituted republic went to ruin. And Sparta did not die alone: the rest of Greece became infected with the same evil contagion which, originating in Sparta, seeped out ever more widely. And do we not have an example closer to home? Did not our own Gracchi brothers, the sons of the great Tiberius Gracchus and grandsons of Africanus, lose their lives in the social strife surrounding their land reform programs?[159]

---

[158] Ephors made up a council of Spartan leaders, who shared power with the dual Spartan kings. Agis was king of Sparta from 244 to 240 B.C. His reform programs (redistribution of land and abolition of debts) were wise and far-sighted, but the aristocracy opposed him and eventually had him executed. He failed where Solon of Athens in his own reforms had succeeded brilliantly.
[159] Tiberius and Caius Gracchus were tribunes who attempted to redistribute land through legislation in the late second century B.C. Their efforts were blocked by the upper classes, and social strife followed.

[81] Aratus Sicyon is rightly praised also.[160] After his city had been held by tyrants for fifty years, he set out for Sicyon from Argos, entered the city in secrecy and took it over. He immediately deposed the tyrant Nicocles and restored six hundred men from exile who had been the city's most opulent men. With his arrival on the scene he liberated his country.

But he quickly became aware of the great difficulties he would have in the matter of property and possessions. He considered it unfair to leave in need those whom he had restored (that is, those whose goods had been previously taken by others); but at the same time, he thought it not quite equitable to reshuffle property rights after the passage of fifty years. This was so because after such a long time, much property had passed into clean hands by inheritances, by deeds of purchase, and by dower. He thus decided neither to order such properties returned, nor to allow the properties to be held rightfully unless the dispossessed were compensated.

[82] When he decided that money was necessary to resolve the problem, he stated that he wanted to travel to Alexandria and that the situation should remain as it was until he returned. He quickly traveled to Ptolemy, his confidant, who was the second king occupying the throne after the founding of Alexandria. He explained to the king that he wanted to liberate his country, and enumerated the relevant issues. Great man that he was, he easily won over the king and obtained a large sum of money from him in the way of assistance.

When he returned to Sicyon, he summoned fifteen of the foremost citizens to a special meeting. He studied the positions of the two sides: those who were holding the property of others and those who had lost property. By a comprehensive valuation of

---

[160] He gained power in the city of Sicyon in 251 B.C. and later became a leader of the Achaean League. Philip of Macedon had him slain in 213 B.C.

these various holdings, he persuaded some that they should prefer a cash settlement to surrender their property claims; and he convinced others that it would be more advantageous to be paid a certain amount, rather than try to pursue an action in litigation. And so it was accomplished that, with domestic concord restored, everyone marched off without a grievance.

[83] What a great and worthy figure was this man born in our country! This is the correct way to treat one's citizens, and not (as we have already seen two times previously) to place an auction-spear in the forum and subject the property of citizens to the cries of the auctioneer. This Greek, because he was a wise and far-seeing leader, thought to take into account the interests of all. This is the highest prudence and wisdom of a good citizen: not to estrange the interests of the population, and to secure all citizens under a spirit of equity. "Let them live under another's roof for free."[161] What is this supposed to mean? That after I have bought, constructed, preserved and poured money into my house, you can enjoy my house against my will? What is this, except to steal something from some and then give it to others?

[84] What arguments can there be for the idea of "wiping the slate clean," except that you may buy an estate with my money? How is it right that you get an estate, but I don't get my money?

XXIV. For this reason we must take care that there is no debt which may act to harm a republic. This evil can be avoided through various methods, but not by permitting the rich to lose their property, and then allowing debtors to gain what belongs to others. Nothing secures a republic more truly than financial good faith, and there can be no such faith unless there exist legal obligations to satisfy debts.

Never was a general forgiveness of debt more strongly urged

---

[161] This is presumably some statement by a politician of whom Cicero disapproves.

than when I was consul. The proposal was encouraged by all types and ranks of men, using even arms and military forces; but I made a stand against them, so that this entire evil was lifted from the shoulders of the republic. Debts were never greater, nor were they ever discharged as easily or cheaply. Once the hope of defrauding creditors was removed, the necessity of working out settlements with them followed. But that man who is the victor now was at one time not a victor; and what he had previously planned, he finally carried through despite it being of scant benefit to him.[162] His taste for committing offenses was such that simply to do harm was for him a pleasure, even if there was no real reason for it.

[85] Therefore, those who guard the state will avoid that type of generosity that takes from some, and gives to others. More than this, they will exert all efforts to see that each person may keep what is his through the impartiality of the laws and the courts, and that neither the poor are defrauded on account of their weakness, nor that jealousy prevents the rich from holding or recovering what belongs to them. In addition, they should work by whatever means possible, either through foreign wars or domestic exertion, to augment the state in power, territory, and revenue. These are the tasks of great men, and these were the things our ancestors accomplished. Those who strive to fulfill these types of duties, which are of the highest benefit to a republic, secure for themselves the greatest thanks and glory.

[86] In these lessons of utility, Antipater of Tyre (who recently died at Athens) believed two things were missed by Panaetius:

---

[162] Another oblique reference to Julius Caesar. Caesar was long suspected (rightly, as it turned out) of intending to reduce the debt burden on the citizenry in some way, either by reducing interest or principal on balances owed. Caesar eventually did pass such a law. Cicero, of course, refuses to ascribe such debt relief legislation by Caesar to any motive grounded in justice, equity or reconciliation.

physical health and financial health.[163] But I believe that this eminent philosopher skipped over these subjects simply because they are too elementary to need much explanation. They are important, of course. But health is sustained by acquaintance with, and regular attention to, one's body; by knowing what things help it, and what irritates it; by upholding continence in all aspects of life and care of the physique (while omitting excessive pleasures); and finally through consultation with those who profess medical knowledge.

[87] One ought to seek money, too, through those means that are free from moral pollution. Money should be saved through diligence and parsimony, and also increased if possible. These subjects were taken up most obligingly by the Socratic philosopher Xenophon in his book entitled *Oeconomicus*. When I was about the age you are now, I translated it from Greek into Latin. But the whole subject of the earning and saving of money (I wish I could add to this the spending of it!) is better handled by any of the important men sitting in the *ianum medium*, than if it were analyzed by any of the philosophers of any school.[164] Nevertheless we must acquaint ourselves with this topic. It is an issued related to utility, which is what we are discussing in this book.

XXV. [88] But it is often necessary to compare different "advantageous" things. This was a fourth topic overlooked by Panaetius. For benefits of the body are accustomed to be

---

[163] Antipater of Tyre was a Stoic philosopher about whom little is known except that he was an acquaintance of Cato and Cicero.

[164] On the north side of the Roman forum were three arched gates called *iani*. These were evenly distributed with one in the middle, called the *ianum medium*. Financial and business matters were conducted in this open air market. The commercial stalls set up for these purposes were called *tabernae*. This same system survives today in many old cities, such as in the covered *souqs* of Aleppo, Cairo and Istanbul.

compared with external benefits (and external benefits with bodily benefits). Physical attributes are also compared with one another, as are external attributes. Bodily advantages are compared with external advantages in this way: whether you would prefer to be healthy, than to be rich. Conversely, external advantages are compared with bodily advantages as follows: whether it is preferable to be rich than to possess the most robust bodily strength.

The physical attributes may be considered among themselves in this way: whether good health should be valued more highly than sensual indulgence, or raw strength over speed. And as for external benefits, we may ponder whether glory should be placed before riches and whether an urban income should be valued more than one derived from farming.

[89] With regard to this type of comparison, Cato the Elder had this to say. When he was asked what would be the best option for a family estate, he replied, "Very good cattle raising." When asked what would be second best after this, he said, "Good enough cattle raising." And third? His answer was, "Not very good cattle raising." What about fourth? "Tilling the soil yourself." And when the interrogator said, "What about lending money?," Cato replied blandly, "What about killing someone?"

From this, and many other things besides, we ought to appreciate the comparative evaluation of different types of expedient things. This fourth category should properly be added to our inquiries on moral duties.

We now proceed to the remaining topics.

COMMENTARY ON BOOK II

Book II builds on the doctrines laid out in the previous book. Many of the topics covered in book II were ones Cicero had personal acquaintance with from his days in politics: the role of fortune, the legal profession, generosity, public service, etc. The book begins on a poignant note (II.1) with his unusually frank explanation of how he came to write on philosophical topics. With the ruin of the republic, he tells us, he was left with little else to do; and rather than let himself be consumed with bitterness and rage, he took to writing.

Human affairs are the outcomes of the interaction between Fortune and social cooperation (II.6). And although man can be a great source of help to his fellows, he can also be a source of harm (II.5). Cicero shows his practical experience in politics when he lists the various reasons why we should help others (II.6), but then takes a surprising turn away from *realpolitik* when he states that love, not fear, is the best kind of motivator (II.7). In this he shows himself so much wiser than Machiavelli, who would have said just the opposite. The methods of repression and fear used by tyrants always becomes self-defeating in the end and historical examples bear this out (II.7—8). The experience of dictators and tyrants in our own time confirm the truth of this.

The discussion of justice and glory (II.9—13) makes us wish that Cicero's lost treatise *De gloria* had been preserved. The best path to glory, he tells us, is the way of justice. All other methods may produce temporary notoriety, but these always fade away in one way or another. The following sections (II.13—22) provide very practical guidance on mentorship, conversation, public speaking, kindness, generosity and the methods by which generosity can be rendered. Here again, Cicero is drawing on his deep experience in politics; then as now, politicians, judges and lawyers were expected to participate in the practical give-and-take of government deal-making.

Cicero reveals himself to be a guardian of conservative interests in II.23 when he discusses land reform. But in II.24 he stumbles when he takes up the subject of debt relief. As he sees it, debt forgiveness amounts to little more than an unjust transfer of wealth from creditors to debtors. He was proud to oppose it, he tells us, on these grounds. This view was likely a natural extension of his belief that a public official was duty-bound to protect the property of citizens. This is odd, since in II.22 (and later in III.22) he shows sympathy for the publicans (tax farmers) in their quest for debt relief from the senate. He strongly criticizes Cato for being inflexible on this issue (III.22) and clearly appreciates how Cato's attitude drove the tax farmers to support Caesar. Like many societies in history, Rome was driven to civil unrest due (at least in part) to its failure to solve the problems of excessive concentrations of wealth, delayed land reforms, and unrelenting political factionalism. Cicero likely understood this on some level but he could never quite bring himself to support a reformer like Caesar who promised radical changes to the existing order. He would always remain a man of tradition. This would prove to be a source of both strength and of weakness.

BOOK III: WHEN MORAL GOODNESS COMES INTO CONFLICT WITH ADVANTAGEOUSNESS

Book III

I. [1] Marcus, my son, remember that Cato the Elder belonged to roughly the same generation as the Publius Scipio who first took the surname Africanus. According to one of Cato's written statements, Scipio said that he himself was never less relaxed than when he was not working, and never less lonely than when he found himself in solitude. This truly is a noble sentiment, and one fitting for a great man and a worthy sage. Scipio's statement reminds us that he used to ponder official business even when at rest and that he was in the habit of commiserating with himself when alone. It shows that he never neglected his duties, and sometimes never even needed to converse with others. The two things that generate laziness in others—leisure and solitude—actually made Scipio sharper.

I would honestly want to be able to say the same thing for myself. But if I am less able to follow such excellence of character by way of imitation, I may at least approach it by desire. Because I am forbidden to pursue the practice of law and elected politics in our republic through the use of unlawful force, I now pursue leisure.[165] Having left the city, I am often now alone, meandering through the countryside.

[2] But I must not compare my leisure with the leisure of Africanus, nor my solitude with his. For he, withdrawing from the official duties of the republic, took some leisure time away from

---

[165] The political turmoil in Rome after the death of Caesar, and the rise of Antony and Octavian, operated to shut down the law courts and republican politics. Cicero was out of power, out of his profession, and despondent.

the outstanding services he was providing for the nation. Sometimes he would undertake to retreat from important meetings with other officials or from large crowds, and find solace in solitude. But my leisure was set up for me by a lack of professional work, not by a desire for tranquility. Once the senate was shuttered and the courts were closed, what worthy activity can I really do in the Curia or in the forum?

[3] So now a man who once lived under the scrutiny of every citizen, and in the aura of the greatest notoriety, now shuns the attentions of the wicked (of whom there are many in this world). I avoid the multitude as much as I can, and am often alone. But I have grasped something from other learned men: when it comes to a choice among bad options, one ought to choose the least harmful one. One should also try to extract something good out of a bad situation. Thus I am making productive use of my leisure time, though it is not quite what someone who rendered special service to the republic deserves. I will not allow this solitude— which necessity and not choice thrust on me--to become a debilitating listlessness.

[4] In any case, Africanus achieved the greater renown, as I see it. There are no monuments in written panegyrics to his character, no work produced by his leisure, and no legacy left of his solitude. We should understand from this that, because of his studies and mental exertions on the issues he was preoccupied with, he had neither been idle nor lonely. But I, who do not have the strength to transport myself out of solitude by silent cogitation, turn myself instead to literary effort. This is why I have written so much more in the short time since the republic fell, than during that long period of my career while the republic still stood.

II. [5] But while all philosophy, dear Cicero, is fecund and fertile, and no part of it desiccated or barren, we can say that no part of it is more fruitful or rewarding than the study of moral duties, from which are gleaned the principles for living a steady and upright life. Although I believe you are hearing and absorbing the teachings of the old masters from Cratippus, the most respected philosopher of our time, I think it beneficial for your ears to be surrounded by such wise voices constantly, if at all possible, and that you hear nothing else.

[6] All of this must be done by anyone who seeks to walk the path of an honest life. And I do not know of anyone who is more suited to this than you. You will have to put up with not a little expectation that you might duplicate my hard work, my path of political offices, and the notoriety of my name. You have taken on a serious responsibility with Cratippus and the Athenians. You will have gained, so to speak, the acquisition of a fine education; to return home with little to show for it would be a disgrace to the honor of Athens and of your instructor. So strive onward as much as your intellect permits, work as much as you can (if learning is a chore and not a pleasure), and do what is necessary to reach your goals. Never let it be said that, after I have made available everything needed, you were lacking in the necessary effort.

But let us move on from this. I have written much for the purpose of encouraging you. We now turn our attention to the remaining part of our discussion of moral propositions.

[7] Panaetius has without doubt discussed most carefully the subject of duties, and I have (with minor adjustments) generally followed him. He has formed three general categories of moral questions about which men might ponder and deliberate:

First, the question of whether what one is doing is morally right or morally wrong. *Second*, whether the act is advantageous or not advantageous.

Third, how to resolve the situation that arises when what appears to be morally right conflicts with what seems advantageous.

On the first two categories of questions he devotes three books. On the third question, however, he did not do what he promised: he assures us he would deal with it in due course, but never does.

[8] I find this surprising, because his student Posidonius writes that Panaetius still lived for thirty years after those books were published. I am further perplexed by the fact that Posidonius only briefly touches on this subject in his writings, especially since he writes that no topic in philosophy is more critical than this one.

[9] I disagree with those who deny that this point was missed by Panaetius, and instead claim that it was "purposely" omitted. These people say that the point would not have needed to be discussed, since advantageousness can never conflict with moral goodness. There is one point that is open to doubt. And this is: whether Panaetius's third category of moral questions[166] should have been included in his discussion, or completely omitted. But another point cannot be doubted: namely, that it may have originally been taken up by Panaetius, but left out of his treatise. When a writer has finished two parts out of a tripartite study, he is glaringly confronted with the unfinished third part. In addition, he promises at the end of the third book that he will examine this subject next.

[10] Posidonius is a reliable corroborating witness to this fact. He mentions in one of his letters that Publius Rutilius Rufus (who studied under Panaetius) used to say that no painter had been found who might finish the incomplete part of the Venus of Cos, which Apelles had left unfinished.[167] The transcendent beauty of her face crushed any hope of creating a comparable likeness for the remainder of her form. In the same way, no one followed through on the topics which Panaetius left unfinished because of the excellence of those things which he did complete.

---

[166] See section [7], immediately preceding.

[167] Apelles was a famous Greek painter. He undertook a painting of Venus for the temple of Aesculapius on the island of Cos, which was said to have been incredibly beautiful. He only finished its head and shoulders before his death. *See* Pliny, Hist. Nat. XXXV.36.79: *Verum omnes prius genitos futurosque postea superavit Apelles Cous*, etc.

III. [11] We cannot, therefore, cast doubt on Panaetius's judgment. It is possible, I suppose, to dispute whether it was right to add this third part to his study on duties. For whether moral rectitude is the only good (as the Stoics maintain), or whether moral rectitude is of such surpassing worth (as our Peripatetics see it) that everything arranged against in on the other side of the scales is inconsequential in comparison, it still cannot be doubted that advantageousness can never compete with moral goodness. We hear that Socrates was in the habit of cursing those who first separated by argument these things that are by nature contiguous. The Stoics are in agreement with this. They believe that whatever is morally right is advantageous, and what is not morally right, is not advantageous.

[12] If Panaetius were the type of man to say that virtue ought to be fostered for its value in bringing us advantage (as do those people who measure the worth of things by the pleasure or absence of pain they bring), he might say that expediency can sometimes conflict with moral goodness. But since he is a man who believes that the only good is what is morally right and that the things which are incompatible with this only *appear* to be advantageous (and neither make life better by their entry nor worse by their departure), it makes no sense that he would have launched into some discussion where he "balances" what seems to be expedient with what is morally right.

[13] It is said by the Stoics that the supreme good is to live in conformity with Nature. I believe that what this means is this: that one should always act consistently with virtue. It also means that, from all those things that are in accord with Nature, one should pick out those things that are not inconsistent with virtue. This being the case, some instructors believe that it is not ethical to make a practical comparison between moral goodness and advantageousness, and that this type of question altogether should not be taught.

Moral rectitude, properly and truly understood, resides only in those who are wise, and it can never be separated from virtue. Those who have not perfected the art of wisdom may adopt the outward *semblance* of moral rectitude, but cannot possess moral rectitude itself.

[14] The Stoics call the duties that we are discussing in these books the "medium" duties.[168] They are universal, and have broad utility. Many good characters adopt them through their own personal integrity and progress in learning. But the duty which the Stoics call "right" is complete and absolute, and as they say, "has all the numbers."[169] It cannot be granted to anyone except the wise man.

[15] However, when something is done in which "medium duties" are implicated, the act is widely seen to be perfect. This is so because the common man is not acquainted with perfection; it is generally outside his range of comprehension. As far as his understanding does go, he believes that nothing is lacking. We see this same dynamic in the critique of poems, paintings and a great many other similar things. The reason why the ignorant enjoy and praise things which should not be praised is, I believe, because there may be something commendable in these art objects which captivates the attention of the ignorant, who remain incapable of perceiving the defects in such works. But when they are instructed by experts, they quickly abandon their flawed opinions.

IV. These duties, then, which we are discussing in these books, the Stoics consider to be a kind of "second-tier" moral rectitude. They are not the exclusive property of wise men, but may be held in general by all types of people. [16] All men having

---

[168] The terms "medium" and "right" duties were previously defined in I.8.
[169] This is a reference to the Pythagoreans, and their belief that numbers had mystical powers. Broadly speaking, they believed that certain numbers (or classes of numbers) were aligned with certain traits or virtues. The expression "having all the numbers" is a way to describe something as more "complete" or virtuous than something else.

an inborn tendency to virtue are moved by these duties. When the two Decii or the two Scipios are remembered as courageous men, or when Fabricius or Aristides are called fair men, the former are not held out as exemplars of fortitude and the latter not as paragons of justice. It is not as if we are reaching for an example of an idealized "wise man." None of these figures were wise men, as the term "wise" may properly be understood. Marcus Cato and Caius Laelius were not wise either, despite being seen as wise and called so by others. Even the great Seven were not wise, although they carried the outward appearance of wise men by their practiced mastery of "medium duties."[170]

[17] Thus, it is not right to compare what is morally good with opposing advantageousness. What we generally call moral goodness, fostered by those who wish to be considered good men, must also not be compared with material benefits. All the same, that moral goodness which falls within our comprehension must be guarded and preserved as dutifully as the pure, unadulterated moral goodness tended to by wise men. If real progress is to be made towards virtue, no other option is possible.

I believe we have said enough regarding those who are thought of as "good" by their close attention to duties.

[18] Those who measure everything by advantages and rewards, and who do not want them to be outweighed by moral goodness, are in the habit of parsing out the various moral implications. They ponder what is expedient and balance these considerations against moral rectitude. Good men are not in the habit of doing this. This is why I believe Panaetius, when he said that men were "accustomed" to balancing these competing factors, was expressing something very specific: he was pointing out that men were "accustomed" to deliberate on such things, and

---

[170] The reference is to the so-called "seven sages" of Greece, who were early statesman and philosophers. *See* Plato's *Protagoras* 342e.

not that they "should" deliberate on them. As a matter of fact, he did not think much of "balancing" morals with expediency. For it is completely corrupt to prefer advantageousness to moral goodness; and it is just as bad to compare them with each other and to hesitate as to which one makes a better choice.

But what is it, then, that sometimes raises doubts for us, and seems to demand additional analysis? I believe it is this: *when a doubt arises regarding some action, we then have to ask what sort of action this really is*.

[19] Often the situation arises when something may normally appear to be morally wrong, but is not in fact morally wrong. To offer an example of this, let us take one that is broadly pertinent: can there be any greater crime than to kill not just any man, but a man who is also an intimate acquaintance? But does the man who has killed a tyrant similarly bind himself to a crime, even if the tyrant was a friend? It does not seem so to the Roman people, who think it the noblest of all great deeds. So, then, does this mean that advantageousness trumps moral goodness? On the contrary: moral goodness *accompanies* advantageousness.

Therefore, we must set up some kind of formula, so that we can judge without error in situations when what we believe is morally good conflicts with what we think is expedient. And if we follow such a formula in comparing these things, we will never fail to obey the call of true duty.

[20] This guideline will be in agreement with the doctrines and teachings of the Stoics, which is what we are generally following in these books. The old Academics and your Peripatetics held at one time the same position on this matter. They placed moral rectitude ahead of what seemed to be advantageous. If these matters are discussed by those who consider moral rectitude also to be advantageous—and nothing is advantageous that is not also morally correct—then we will see better results than if these matters are discussed by those who believe that something *not* advantageous may be morally correct,

and that something *not* morally correct may be advantageous. But the doctrine of our Academy gives us great freedom to defend whatever may be the most likely solution to a problem. I will now return to the guideline spoken of earlier.

V. [21] To take something away from another and to increase one's position through the disadvantage of someone else is more contrary to Nature than death, poverty, pain or all the other unfortunate things that can afflict the body or our material goods. When this happens, it takes away the bonds of intimacy between people and society. If we become so infected with this destructive ethic, that to gain a benefit we will steal from another, or violate another then the fabric of society which most adheres to Nature's laws will be torn.

[22] If each of our bodily organs got the idea that for the sake of its own well-being it should siphon off the nutrition of a neighboring member, then our entire body would become debilitated and perish. In the same way, if each one of us snatched the resources of others and made off with whatever he could to use for his own benefit, then it is certain that human society and community would be turned upside down. It is allowed and not offensive to Nature, for a man to prefer to earn life's necessities for himself, rather than to earn them for others; but Nature does not tolerate the augmenting of our own resources, wealth and power by plundering others.

[23] We see this not only in Nature (i.e., the universal laws of mankind), but also in the codified laws of nations through which republics are sustained as cohesive entities. It is established as accepted doctrine that one may not harm another for the sake of his own benefit. This is the principle that the laws watch over. This is what the laws aim for: that the common fellowship of citizens should remain intact and that anyone trying to destroy this fellowship should face condemnation, imprisonment, exile or death.

The universal rule of Nature, which is essentially divine and human law, brings this about much more than we appreciate. Whoever wishes to submit to this principle (and all who wish to live in accordance with Nature will submit to it) will never commit the sin of hungering for what belongs to others, nor of using for himself what he has stolen from others.

[24] As a matter of fact, loftiness and greatness of spirit and indeed generosity, justice and liberality are much more in accordance with Nature than are the enjoyment of pleasures, wealth or even life. But it is for a great and lofty spirit indeed to look down on these things and to consider them of little worth when comparing them to the common good. To take something unlawfully from another and to use it for one's own advantage is more contrary to Nature than death, pain or other similar things of this type.

[25] Likewise it is more in accordance with Nature to seek to imitate Hercules, if possible, and to assume the greatest labors and troubles for the sake of preserving and securing the future of all mankind. Better to do this than to live in solitude without any troubles, while frolicking in pleasures and abounding in great wealth with the goal of trying to surpass others in beauty and strength. Hercules's reputation and the grateful memory of his services have accorded him a place in the pantheon of the gods.

And so, he who has the best and most brilliant character will count a life of service to be more fitting than a life of self-indulgent inactivity. It must also be concluded from this that a man obedient to the law of Nature will be unable to harm another man.

[26] He who violates another man in order to obtain an advantage for himself either believes that he is not doing anything contrary to Nature's laws or he thinks that it is more justifiable to avoid death, poverty, pain or even the deprivation of children, family members or friends, than it is to inflict an injury on someone else. If someone thinks that the violating of other men in society is not a sin against the law of Nature, what is there really

to discuss with the type of person who takes from a man his masculine identity? But if he believes that this type of conduct should be shunned and that the other options are indeed worse (i.e., death, poverty and pain), he still would be making a mistake to suppose that sins against the body or against property are more serious than sins against the soul.[171]

VI. Therefore, this one proposition ought to be the objective of all men: that what is advantageous to a single citizen and what is advantageous to the group as a whole should be the same. When one person takes for himself with disregard for the common welfare, the connective tissues of fellowship among citizens are dissolved.

[27] And so if Nature directs that one man should offer help to another man simply because he is a fellow-man, whoever he may be, on account of this same motive then it necessarily follows that this common advantage is in accordance with Nature. If this is so, we are all governed by one and the same law of Nature. And if this statement itself is true, then we are prohibited from violating another person by the law of Nature. Since the first proposition is true, the last one must also be true.

[28] For it is indeed absurd to say, as some do, that they would take nothing wrongfully from their parents or siblings to use for their own benefit, but would apply a quite different rule with regard to the rest of their fellow citizens. These people maintain that no law and no social bonds exist for the sake of the common welfare among citizens. This sentiment pulls apart all sense of social order in a state. Those who advocate for the human rights

---

[171] This is a difficult (and possibly corrupt) sentence in the original. It makes more sense if one reads the text as *et multo illa peiora, mortem, paupertatem, dolorem, errat in eo, quod ullum aut corporis aut fortunae vitium vitiis animi gravius existimat* rather than *sed multo illa peiora, mortem,* etc. Preferring the reading that makes the first word *et* instead of *sed* is more consistent with the meaning of the preceding sentences.

of citizens, but deny those rights when it comes to foreigners, destroy the common fellowship of mankind. Once honorable treatment for all is taken away, kindness, goodness and justice are without exception destroyed. Those who carry out this sort of destruction must be judged as profoundly offensive to the immortal gods. Such people bring the established social order among men to ruin. For the tightest bond of the social order is that we consider it more against Nature for one man to take from another for his own benefit, than it is to suffer any kind of personal harm, whether it be to one's body, property or even one's soul. Harms of this sort are inconsequential when compared with justice; for justice is by far the most important virtue, the empress and mistress of them all.

[29] Perhaps someone will say something like this: "Would it be right for a wise man suffering from starvation to take food from another man who is a useless good-for-nothing?" This would certainly not be right. My physical life is not as important to me as is the health of my soul, which commands me to hurt no one for the sake of my own benefit. Do we need another example? May a good man, to prevent himself from freezing, rob an article of clothing from the cruel and merciless tyrant Phalaris?[172]

[30] These examples may be decided without difficulty. If you take something even from a good-for-nothing person and use it for your own benefit, then you are doing something inhuman and contrary to Nature's law. But what if, on the other hand, you went about your life and were able to take something from another person, and you were truly acting on behalf of the greatest interests of the state and human society? Then there would be no blame attached to this deed.

---

[172] Phalaris was the tyrant of the Sicilian city of Acragas (Agrigento) from 570 to 554 B.C. He was notorious for his cruelty, and is said to have constructed a huge bronze bull for the purpose of roasting alive his condemned.

If this were not one's true motivation, then such a thief must bear the burden of the wrongs he has caused rather than steal something from someone else. Sickness, need and similar types of physical evils are not more against the law of Nature than are the evils of appropriating and coveting the goods of another. The neglect of the common good is also against Nature; it is patently unjust.

[31] Therefore, this same law of Nature, which sustains and preserves the interests of mankind, will certainly ordain that the necessities of life are transferred from an unproductive and useless man to a man who is wise, good and strong. If such a good man perished, it would remove a great amount of value from his community's common benefit. If this must be done, however, he should not think that an inflated sense of conceit or narcissism can be an excuse to inflict a harm on someone else. In the performance of his duty the wise man will take into account what is relevant to his community's advantage and, as I often make a point of mentioning, the good of human society in general.

[32] One can easily decide the hypothetical example we posed earlier regarding Phalaris. We can have no alliance with tyrants; rather, there can only be the most emphatic severance of ties. It is not contrary to Nature to steal from such a man, or even if possible to kill him, if we may speak honestly. All such types of pestilence and immoral human dregs should be removed from civil society by force. Just as limbs are amputated if they start to become bloodless and diseased and harm the other organs of the body, so also should an animal in human form, a savage beast, be cut out, as it were, from the "body" of human society.

All these duty-related questions are ethical problems of this type. We must examine what duties are appropriate to each situation.

VII. [33] I believe that Panaetius would have pursued more inquiries along these lines, had not some undisclosed reason or accident barred his way from doing so. A good many topics in this vein are discussed in his earlier books. From these books one is able to see what must be avoided due to its moral indecency, and what should not be avoided (because it is not morally corrupt).

Our work is not yet done, although it can be considered as approaching completion. We are placing the pointed gable on the house, so to speak. And just as the geometricians are not in the habit of teaching every little theorem, but rather demand that certain propositions be conceded as self-evident so they can explain their conclusions more easily, so I propose to you, my dear Cicero[173] that you grant me, if you can, the basic proposition that *nothing should be aspired to for its own sake except that which is morally right*. But even if Cratippus does not take this stance, I am sure you will agree with the statement that what is morally correct is certainly worth pursuing for its own sake. For me, either one of these choices is sufficient; either this one or that one seems more probable.[174] In any case, no other options seem likely.

[34] Panaetius should be defended on this point. He did not say that advantageous things could conflict with things that are morally good, since such a viewpoint was not part of his belief system. He only said that things that were *apparently* advantageous could conflict with moral goodness. He often insists that nothing is advantageous that is not also morally sound, and nothing that is morally sound is not similarly advantageous. No greater evil has insinuated itself into the life of man, he says, than

---

[173] Referring to his son Marcus, as noted previously.

[174] When Cicero says "either one" of these choices or options, he is referring to these two alternatives: whether moral goodness was the only thing worth seeking for its own sake, or whether there were other things in addition to moral goodness that were worth seeking for their own sake (e.g., health). Cratippus (according to Cicero) apparently believed that moral goodness was *not* the only thing worth seeking for its own sake.

the idea that we should separate the "morally good" from the "advantageous."

Thus, in order that we might not put advantageousness before moral goodness, and that we might judge these two factors correctly, Panaetius introduced an apparent (but not a real) contradiction between the two factors in case they should ever clash with each other. This remaining part of our study[175] we will complete without the help of any predecessors, but rather as the saying goes, "by our own fighting spirit."[176] Nothing published on this subject since the time of Panaetius seems to be very satisfactory, at least judging from what has found its way into my hands.

VIII. [35] When one is presented with something expedient, one is unavoidably tempted by it. But if you pay attention to your heart, you may see that there is some moral disgrace attached to that very thing that appears expedient. Expediency is not exactly abandoned; rather, one perceives that expediency is not really possible when it is tainted by moral degradation. If nothing is so contrary to Nature as moral corruption (Nature seeks right, consistency and constancy and rejects the opposites of these qualities), and nothing is so in accordance with Nature as advantageousness, then it clearly follows that advantageousness and moral corruption cannot exist simultaneously in the same thing.

So, if we have been brought into this world for the purpose of attaining moral rectitude, and that alone is worth aspiring to (as Zeno believed), or at least if moral rectitude has more relative value than everything else (as Aristotle insisted), then we must

---

[175] The "remaining part" being the moral conflict issues not discussed by Panaetius.

[176] The phrase used here is *Marte nostro*, or literally, "with our Mars," meaning with the help of the god of war. Knowledge must be gained through struggle.

conclude that moral rectitude is either the *only* good or the *highest* good. That which is good, is definitely advantageous; thus, whatever is morally right is also advantageous.

[36] Here we see a common mistake of the person with a flawed character: when he sees something that appears to be advantageous, he immediately jumps at it and disconnects it from what is morally right. This is how evil-intentioned daggers, poisons and maliciously false testimonies are born. This same impulse also gives rise to larceny, fraud, defalcation while acting as a fiduciary and the shameless exploitation of allies and fellow citizens. It produces the desire for excessive wealth, for usurping power, and finally for playing lord and master over a free people. Nothing more foul or wicked can be imagined than these sorts of bad acts. Acting under the influence of flawed judgment and wishful thinking, the people who do these things see only the imagined benefits that they might get; they do not see the inevitable punishment that results. And when I say punishment, I do not mean punishment under the law, which they often evade, but instead *the very bitter punishment that is a consequence of moral corruption.*

[37] For this reason, then, this class of deliberations is best tossed aside completely. It is appropriate only for criminals or similarly corrupt people, the type of people who spend time pondering whether to do what is morally right or whether to contaminate themselves by doing what they know to be bad acts. A wicked deed exists in the very act of deliberation, even if the crime itself is never done. These competing interests must not be "weighed" at all. The very act of deliberation itself is morally disgraceful.

In every deliberation, we must get rid of the idea and expectation that we can hide or conceal a wicked act. If indeed we have learned anything in philosophy, it should be enough for us to realize that, even if we can conceal our crimes from gods and men, we still must never do anything motivated by impulses of greed, injustice, caprice or intemperance.

IX. [38] To make this point, the tale of Gyges was introduced by Plato.[177] When a fissure opened up in the earth after a series of rains, Gyges descended into it. There he found a bronzed horse, as the fables say; and in its side he saw a folding door. Inside the horse he saw the body of a dead man of huge proportions, with a gold ring on his finger. He removed the ring and put it on his own finger. He was the shepherd of a king, and so he then went to a general meeting of shepherds. When he turned the ring's bezel towards the palm of his hand, he was seen by no one, while he himself was able to see everything.[178] When he rotated the ring back to its original position on his finger, he again was able to be seen by other people.

So, taking advantage of the opportunity created by this magic ring, he seduced the queen of Lydia and, with her as his accomplice, murdered the king of that country. He destroyed all whom he thought might oppose him, and neither was anyone able to see him as he went about these crimes. Thus, with the unexpected help of the ring he rose to become king of Lydia. But if a wise man had such a ring, he would no more think he could commit crimes than if he did not have it. For moral goodness and not secrecy for evil deeds is what good men seek.

[39] About this story, some philosophers—certainly not bad men, yet not very bright—claim that this allegory told by Plato was invented or embellished. As if Plato ever promoted the story as a factual matter or as something even possible! Herein lies the power of the magic ring concept and of this little fable: if no one were able to know or suspect when you do something for the sake of riches, power, domination or sensual pleasure, and if such an action could be forever hidden from gods and men, would you do it?

---

[177] The story of Gyges is found in *Republic* II.359C. It also appears in Herodotus (I.8-11).

[178] I.e., the ring gave the shepherd the power of invisibility.

They deny that this scenario is possible. And yet it is indeed possible. So I ask those who think this hypothetical is impossible: if it *were* possible, what would you do? The doubters truly continue to bear down on me clumsily: they deny that this hypothetical is "possible," and smugly stick to this. Whatever value my words may have as a thought experiment, they do not see. When we ask them what choice they would make if they *could* permanently conceal a wicked act, we are not asking them whether it is *physically possible* to conceal a wicked act.

Introducing this little thought-experiment is like torture to them. If they answer that they could indeed commit an evil act with impunity (i.e., to do what is most expedient for them), then they are basically admitting that they have bad characters. But if they deny that they could commit an undetected evil deed, then they are, in effect, conceding that all morally wrong things must without exception be avoided.

Let us now return to our original proposition.

X. [40] Many situations arise which agitate our minds with the outward appearance of expediency. When we think about it, however, we see the real issue is not whether moral goodness will be abandoned because of the great attractiveness of the competing expediency (since that would be immoral), but rather whether the expedient thing can be gained without moral disgrace. When Brutus abolished the authority of his associate Collatinus, the action was widely held to be unjust.[179]

Collatinus had been an ally of Brutus during the expulsion of the monarchy; he had been Brutus's right-hand man, and had provided valuable counsel. But when the leadership element of the country decided that the family of Superbus, the Tarquin clan, and the institution of the monarchy itself should be abolished, then

---

[179] Lucius Tarquinius Collatinus was elected co-consul with Lucius Junius Brutus. *See* Livy II.2.

what was advantageous (i.e., to act as political counselor) was also so morally right that Collatinus ought to have promptly reconciled himself to the decision. So, in this situation, advantageousness prevailed because it was also morally right. Without this element of moral goodness, there could have been no advantageousness.

[41] But in the case of the king[180] who founded Rome the situation was different. The appearance of expediency was what drove his mind. For when it seemed to him more advantageous to rule Rome alone than with someone else, he killed his brother.[181] He abandoned his goodness and his humanity, so that he might get what he thought was advantageous, but was not. He cited the matter of Rome's wall as the pretext for what he did; but this was only an empty display of moral goodness, neither justifiable nor defensible. Let me say it openly: he committed a grave offense, whether we are talking about Romulus or Quirinus.[182]

[42] We should not, however, disregard our own self-interests, and hand over to others the things we require for ourselves. Each man must take care of his own interest, insofar as it does not injure another. Recall the wise words (among many) of Chrysippus, when he said: "He who runs in an athletic race ought to compete and struggle as intensely as he can. But in order to win, he ought not to trip or push over a fellow competitor. So in life, it is not unjust for a man to seek what he needs for his own use; but to steal something away from someone else is, in fact, unjust."[183]

---

[180] I.e., Romulus.

[181] In the legend of the two brothers who founded Rome (Romulus and Remus), Romulus supposedly killed Remus in a quarrel. The source of the quarrel was related to the location and boundary of the city. Romulus preferred to set the city on one hill (Palatine), and Remus another (the Aventine).

[182] Quirinus was an early god of the Roman state. So what Cicero means metaphorically here is "whether we are talking about a god or a man."

[183] Chrysippus of Soli (c. 280—207 B.C.) was the third head of the Stoic school after the death of Cleanthes.

[43] Duties are greatly muddled when it comes to friends. Not to do for them what you can is contrary to duty, and to do for them what is not equitable is also contrary to duty. But there is a short and simple piece of advice for these types of situations. Things which are considered expedient, such as political honors, riches, sensual pleasures and other things of this sort, should never take priority over our friends. But for a friend's sake, a good man will do nothing against his country's interest, his oath or his personal honor, not even if he happens to be the judge in a friend's case. He suspends his status as a friend, and assumes the duties of a judge. He will make some allowance for friendship, in that he will prefer his friend's case to be the truth, all other things being equal. And he may accommodate his friend in granting him as much time as is needed to argue his case that the law will allow.

[44] When the time comes for sentence of judgment to be rendered, he will remember to summon God as his witness. This is, I argue, his own power of reason; and God has granted man nothing more divine than this. If we can only maintain it, we have already received a splendid custom from our ancestors: that is, charging jurors with the instruction, "Do what you can, using good faith." This motto is applicable to the situation that I just a bit earlier talked about, namely, when a judge can ethically make an allowance on behalf of a friend. If we are obliged to do everything our friends want, then we must realize that these relationships are not friendships, but conspiracies.

[45] However, I am speaking here of regular friendships; among wise and outstanding men this type of situation cannot exist.[184] They say that the Pythagorean disciples Damon and Phintias had just this kind of pure friendship.[185] When the tyrant

---

[184] I.e., the situation described in the preceding paragraph, where a friend can lure another into a conspiracy, or some other situation where too much is being demanded.

[185] This famous story is also mentioned by Cicero in *Tusc. Disp.* V.22.

Dionysius fixed an execution date for one of these two, the one who had been marked for death requested a few days to get his personal affairs in order. The other one was designated as a surety in the condemned man's absence. If the convicted man did not return to face sentence, the surety would have to forfeit his own life instead. When the convicted man returned as promised on the day of sentence, the astonished tyrant was so moved by their fidelity to each other that he sought to become a third party to the friendship between them.

[46] So, when what seems to be advantageous in friendship is compared to what is morally good, we ought to disregard the appearance of expediency and value more highly what is morally good instead. And when inappropriate things are demanded in a friendship, higher moral obligations and fidelity to principles should take precedence over personal friendship. *This is how the analysis must be done when conflicting duties are being compared.*

XI. Under the appearance of expediency, wrongs are very often committed in affairs of state, as in our destruction of Corinth. Harsher still was the decision of the Athenians who ordered that the Aeginetans, who possessed a strong fleet, should submit to having their thumbs amputated.[186] This action was considered advantageous because Aegina, due to its proximity to the Piraeus, was too much of a military threat. But nothing so cruel can be advantageous. Cruelty is greatly offensive to human nature, and Nature is what we ought to be guided by.

[47] It is also bad to act as Pennus did in olden times and Papius did more recently: that is, to bar foreigners from access to

---

[186] The origin of this story is not clear, and it may be spurious. Aegina is an island in the Saronic Gulf and the incident is supposed to have occurred in the Peloponnesian War, but it is not found in Thucydides.

one's city and to expel those within its borders.[187] It may not be right for one who is not a citizen to be accorded the benefits of citizenship; certainly the legal doctrines of the wise consuls Scaevola and Crassus argue in favor of this point. Yet to prohibit a foreigner from making use of a city is clearly inhumane.

There are clear examples of situations where the appearance of "national expediency"[188] has counted for little, when weighed against moral goodness. Our history is full of such examples, with perhaps the best being found in the history of the Second Punic War. Once the news of the unmitigated disaster at Cannae became known, our nation revealed a greater fortitude than that displayed during any of her victories.[189] There was no display of fear and no talk of making a settlement with the enemy. Such is the power of moral rectitude, that it overpowers the limp appearance of expediency.

[48] During the Persian invasion of Greece, the Athenians were unable to stem the tide of the enemy.[190] Abandoning the city, they sent their women and children to safety at Troezen and, taking to their warships, prosecuted the war for Greek freedom by naval power. A man named Cyrsilus recommended that they remain at Athens and receive Xerxes when he arrived; in response the Athenians stoned him to death. His suggestion seemed to be expedient, but it was not. It was, instead, repugnant to moral goodness.

---

[187] Marcus Junius Pennus, as tribune of the plebs in 126 B.C., proposed to expel all foreigners from Rome. Caius Papius, tribune in 65 B.C., tried to do the same thing.

[188] *Illa praeclara, in quibus publicae utilitatis species prae honestate contemnitur.* The *illa* here is short for *illa exempla.* "National expediency" could also be "public utility" or "public expediency," and refers to what is in the national interest.

[189] The Roman defeat at Cannae by Hannibal in the Second Punic War was one of the most severe in its history. Estimates of the dead run from fifty to seventy thousand.

[190] The invasion of Xerxes in 480 B.C.

181

[49] Themistocles, after the conclusion of his victorious war with Persia, said in a speech to the Athenian Assembly that he had a plan to restore the state to health, but that it was not necessary to reveal his plan. He proposed that the people appoint a representative with whom he might have a dialogue about his plan. Aristides was chosen for this task. Themistocles told him that the Spartan fleet, which had been led to Gytheum, could be secretly burned; and if this were done, Spartan power would certainly be broken. When Aristides heard this, he came to the Assembly with great expectations, and said that while Themistocles's plan may have been very advantageous, it was in no way morally good. So the Athenians finally reckoned that what was not morally good was also not expedient. With the endorsement of Aristides they also rejected out of hand, and would not listen to, any similar proposals. Better than us were these men! For we allow pirates to plunder openly, yet insist on levying taxes on our allies.[191]

XII. We conclude from all this that what is morally wrong can never be advantageous, even when one gains something that he believes is advantageous. *To believe that a morally corrupt thing can be expedient is truly a ruinous concept.*

[50] Nevertheless, as I said earlier, situations often happen when advantageousness seems to conflict with moral rectitude. When this happens, it must be decided whether the conflict is incurable, or whether expediency may be married, so to speak, with moral rectitude. These are the types of inquiries I am talking about.

---

[191] These are oblique criticisms of Caesar, and praises of Pompey. Early in his career Pompey had achieved fame for ridding the Mediterranean of pirates. Piracy made a comeback in the turbulent years of the civil war between Pompey and Caesar. The comment about "levying taxes on allies" refers to Caesar's habit of exacting tribute from regional rulers who had taken Pompey's side during the war.

Suppose, for example, a good man is sailing from Alexandria to Rhodes with a large cargo of grain during a time of scarcity, famine and extremely high food prices. Suppose also that this man knows other merchants after him are headed for Rhodes, laden with foodstuffs. Should he tell the Rhodians about the other ships, or should he keep silent, and sell his food at the highest price he can? In this example we have imagined that our subject is a wise and good man. We are trying to inquire into the thought process and mental workings of the kind of man who would not conceal such critical information from the Rhodians, yet might still doubt that such concealment could be morally wrong.[192]

[51] In hypotheticals of this type, we commonly see two different views: one advocated by Diogenes of Babylon, a great and influential Stoic, and another advanced by his follower Antipater, a quite brilliant man in his own right.[193] Antipater would say that all material information should be disclosed, so that the buyer knows everything the seller knows.

According to Diogenes, a merchant ought to represent to the buyer any defects in his goods, insofar as the applicable civil law may require him to do so; but as long as he is not dishonest in the act of selling, he may otherwise do as he wishes. Since his business is selling, he may rightly try to get the best price he can. Diogenes's merchant would say, "I have brought my goods to market, and have offered them for sale. I sell my goods at prices not higher than anyone else's, and perhaps even at lower prices when the market supply is great. How is anyone being hurt?"

---

[192] This is artfully expressed. Here Cicero considers it self-evident that price-gouging during a famine is morally wrong. So he does not even bother trying to argue against those who would assert the contrary. He takes the subtler approach and addresses the majority of people: those who would do the right thing, yet might still be secretly tempted to profit from the misery of others.

[193] Diogenes was a student of Chrysippus in Athens. Antipater of Tarsus was the instructor of Panaetius.

[52] Antipater's reasoning from the other side would be this: "What are you saying? You ought to be mindful of the needs of your fellow-men and serve the interests of human society. You were born under this law and contain within you the principles of Nature; you should submit to their control and follow them. Your expediency should be the community's expediency, and likewise the community's expediency should be yours. Will you deceive your fellow-men about relief supplies that are heading their way?"

Perhaps here Diogenes would then say: "To conceal is one thing, but to remain silent is something quite different. If I don't reveal to you the nature of the gods, or the meaning of life, I'm not concealing anything from you.[194] Knowing these things would be of more value to you than to know the current price of wheat. I am not required to tell you everything that may be advantageous for you to hear."

[53] Antipater might fire back, "You *absolutely are* required to tell me, if you are being mindful of the bonds made by Nature that connect all people in human society."

"I am mindful of them," the advocate for Diogenes would reply. "But what sort of society is this, where no one can be an unqualified owner of anything? If this is how you see it, a merchant should not even bother to sell things, but instead should just give them away!"

XIII. You can see in this entire debate that neither side says: "Although this action is morally wrong, nevertheless, because it is expedient, I am still going to do it." Rather, one side says that the proposed action is expedient, and not morally wrong; and the other side says that the proposed action, because it is morally wrong, must not be done.

----

[194] I have chosen to render *finis bonorum* ("ultimate good," or "highest good") as "meaning of life" here, since its colloquial feel is more appropriate in this passage.

[54] Imagine that a good man wants to sell a house due to some defect he knows about, but of which others are ignorant. It may be pestilential but, in outward appearance, very sanitary. People may not know that pests are hidden in every room, or that defective and shoddy materials were used in construction. Suppose no one but the owner knows these things. I then ask you: if the seller does not reveal these things to prospective buyers, and sells the house for more than he thinks he would otherwise get, has he acted unjustly or dishonestly?

[55] Antipater would say, "He certainly has acted dishonestly. For this amounts to refusing to show a lost man the right road; in Athens such conduct is punishable by a public sanction. To allow a home buyer to meet with such trickery and suffer financial loss: is this not the very same thing? In fact it is worse than not showing someone the right road; it is inducing another to believe erroneous information."

Here is Diogenes with the ready response: "Has this man, who did not even encourage you, forced you to buy his house? What he did not want, he advertised for sale. What you wanted, you bought. If someone who advertises a property as a "good and well-built home" is not considered to be committing fraud when the property is neither good nor well-built, then those who do not overtly praise their homes are even less culpable.[195] Where there is conscious judgment on the part of a buyer, how can there be any seller's fraud? But if not every part of a representation has to be perfect, do you think that what *has not* been represented should also be perfect? Be realistic about this! What could be more idiotic than for a vendor to expound on all the flaws in the goods he is trying to sell! And what could be more ridiculous than a real estate auctioneer who announces at the seller's instruction: "Pest-ridden house for sale"!

---

[195] I.e., those who stand silent and say nothing are less guilty than those who use puffery in advertising.

[56] Clearly, then, in certain ambiguous scenarios, the argument for moral goodness can be made on the one hand, and on the other hand, one can make the case for expediency. Sometimes the case for expediency can be laid out in such a way that it is equated with moral goodness; and, conversely, not to do the expedient thing can be portrayed as a moral shortcoming. This is the conflict that is often seen to take place between advantageousness and moral rectitude. These cases must be decided. I did not pose these examples as random thought-experiments, but rather as opportunities for resolving real ethical problems.

[57] Therefore, I believe that neither the grain-merchant should have concealed material facts from the people of Rhodes, nor should the house-seller have so behaved to the prospective home-buyer. For concealment does not consist in simply being silent; it is found, rather, in situations where one party knows something that is material to the transaction in question, yet wants to keep silent about it for the sake of his own gain. Who does not see what sort of dissimulation this may be in practice, and what type of person would do it? Certainly it would not be someone who is open, unaffected, frank, just, or a good man; rather, it would be someone wily, dark, cunning, mendacious, treacherous, roguish, devious or cynical with old age. Is it not inexpedient to be tagged with these adjectives for vice, and maybe even with other worse labels?

XIV. [58] If blame is to fall on those who leave things unsaid, what should we think of those who make a habit of saying deceitful things? Caius Canius, a refined and well-educated man, visited the city of Syracuse for leisure, and not, as he used to say, for the sake of doing business. He mentioned to some people that he wanted to buy a piece of property, where he could invite his friends and relax without having to deal with annoying distractions.

When word of this got around, a banker from Syracuse named

Pythius informed Canius that, while he did not have such an estate for sale, he did have one that Canius could use, if he wanted. He also invited Canius to have dinner with him at the estate the next day, which he agreed to. Pythius, who as a banker could call in favors from all classes of people, rounded up some fishermen and asked them to fish the next day in front of his estate. He told them specifically how to behave.

Canius came at the agreed time for dinner, and a lavish banquet had been prepared by his host. A large number of boats were in the plain view of the diners.[196] Each fisherman brought what he had caught from the sea and laid the fish at Pythius's feet.

[59] Canius said, "Can you tell me what's going on here, Pythius? What's with all this fish? And all these boats?"

Pythius responded, "What makes you think something strange is happening? This is where all the fish of Syracuse are, and this is where all the fresh water is drawn. This villa is a necessity for these men."

Canius was now very interested in the villa; with his desire mounting he asked Pythius to sell it to him. At first Pythius put him off. I will not go into all the details of the negotiations, but eventually Canius got what he wanted. A desirous man of abundant resources paid what Pythius asked, and even bought the villa's furnishings. He recorded the ledger-entry and wound up the sale.

The next day, Canius invited his friends to his new house. He himself arrived early. There was nothing there, not even an oarlock. He inquired of a neighbor whether there was some holiday for fishermen, because he could see no one on the water.

"None that I am aware of," the neighbor answered. "But nobody ever really comes here to fish anyway. That's why I was surprised at what happened yesterday."

---

[196] This is obviously a seaside estate, overlooking the water.

Canius was now boiling with rage. But what should he do? My colleague and good friend, the jurist Caius Aquilius, had not yet drafted the statutes for commercial fraud.[197] Regarding this kind of fact pattern, when Aquilius was asked what constituted fraud he would answer: "A condition arising when certain representations have been proffered, but something materially different has been delivered."[198] This is certainly a brilliant definition and one pronounced by a recognized authority. Pythius, therefore, and all others who say one thing but do another, are morally corrupt, perfidious and deceitful. No deed that they do can be considered expedient, since their actions are poisoned with underhandedness.

XV. [61] If Aquilius's definition is true, then false representation and dissimulation must be banished from all parts of our lives. In this way a good man will neither falsely represent anything, nor hide any material fact, in order to buy or sell on favorable terms. Malicious fraud had already been a punishable offense under the existing laws. Guardianships under the original Twelve Tables, and fraud against minors under the Plaetorian Law,[199] are examples of this; the same principle is observed in situations where no specific law is invoked, yet where the admonition "in good faith" is inscribed on legal documents.

In other types of cases different words make prominent appearances. In the matter of a dispute over a newlywed's dowry, we find the motto "the fairer is the better;" or in litigation over

---

[197] Caius Aquilius Gallus was praetor in 67 B.C. and a colleague of Cicero. He was responsible for significant reforms to the legal code, especially with regard to commercial fraud. These rules for dealing with fraud became known as *formulae de dolo malo* ("general forms on fraud").

[198] The wording of Aquilius's definition is terse: *cum esset aliud simulatum, aliud actum*. A legalistic translation of this sentence fits the context well here.

[199] The *lex Plaetoria* defined minors as those under twenty-five years of age, and protected them from exploitation by fraud.

fiduciary duties, we see "good conduct among good people." So what do you conclude from this? Can there be any component of fraud in the guidance provided by the motto "the fairer is the better"? When a phrase like "good conduct among good people" is solemnized, can anything deceitful or malicious be contemplated? As Aquilius says, "fraud in the inducement" is initiated with the act of false representation.

All false representation, therefore, must be shunned in business dealings. A seller must not make use of a sham bidder at an auction to pump up prices; and a buyer must not use one to suppress true market values, either. Each party, when the time comes to name his price, need not speak more than once.[200]

[62] Indeed, once Quintus Scaevola (son of Publius Scaevola) inquired into the value of a piece of property that he intended to buy. The seller disclosed it. Scaevola retorted that it was worth more, and promptly added one hundred thousand sesterces to the purchase price![201] No one denies that this had been the act of a good man. They do deny it was the act of a commercially savvy man; just as it would have been if, for example, Scaevola had sold the property for less than he might have gotten. These are part and parcel of the paradoxes of life, by which some men are reckoned "good" and others "wise." With this fact in mind, Ennius tells us,

---

[200] Such attempts to manipulate market prices for equities and real estate are of old date. Despite modern laws meant to regulate stock markets and insider dealings, "pump and dump" schemes still do happen. Sellers attempt to generate momentum and excitement in an asset by repeated fake bids, thereby "pumping up" the price.

[201] In the time of the republic, the *sestertius* was a silver coin valued at one-quarter of a *denarius* and one-hundredth of an *aureus*. Trying to calculate relative values of currencies over a long time span is not easy. In 2015 US dollars, the value of a *sestertius* was probably about $1.55 and that of a *denarius* about $5.00.

He whose wisdom brings him no advantage acquires his knowledge in vain.

And this saying is surely true, as long as Ennius's understanding of "advantage" harmonizes with my own.

[63] In Hecaton of Rhodes's books on moral duties which he, as a follower of Panaetius, dedicated to Quintus Tubero,[202] I have read passages stating that "the wise man should do nothing to violate customs, laws or respected institutions, but should instead focus on his own personal affairs.[203] We do not wish to be rich solely for our own sake, but also for our children, families, friends and finally for our country. The aggregate skills of individuals are the collective wealth of the state."

Hecaton would in no way have approved of the real estate "negotiations" of Quintus Scaevola, which I mentioned in the preceding section. This is because Hecaton says he will only desist from doing those things for his own personal advantage that are specifically forbidden by statute. This type of attitude merits neither our approval nor our respect.

[64] But if false pretenses or hiding relevant facts constitute fraud, then there are few things in which fraud is not somehow implicated. If someone is a good person, who benefits from transactions when he can, yet does no one any harm, then certainly we will not easily find out about this type of good person. Therefore, it is never expedient to commit a moral wrong, because such a wrong is always indecent. And because it is always morally good to be a good man, it is always advantageous to be a good man.

XVI. [65] In our body of civil law pertaining to real property, it is required that sellers disclose to buyers all defects in the

---

[202] Quintus Aelius Tubero was a nephew of Scipio Africanus the Younger.

[203] A Stoic philosopher (fl. 100 B.C.) about whom almost nothing is known.

property that are known to exist. Under the old Laws of the Twelve Tables, the practice was to fix any defects that were specifically noted. Defects that the seller concealed would be subject to a penalty equal to twice the amount of damages incurred. Modern judges have established a similar sanction for failing to disclosure a material defect. They have established case law mandating that, if a seller knows of any material defect in his property, he ought to fix it unless the defect has first been disclosed expressly and unequivocally to the buyer.

[66] When some augurs[204] were about to perform a reading from a hilltop and ordered Tiberius Claudius Centumalus, who owned an apartment house on the Caelian Hill, to tear it down because it was blocking the augurs from making their readings, Claudius sold his building. This was then bought by Publius Calpurnius Lanarius. The augurs then presented the same demolition request to the new owner. Calpurnius then removed the obstructing parts of the building; but he also learned that Claudius had advertised the house for sale only *after* he had been ordered by the augurs to tear down parts of it.

He then filed a civil complaint against Claudius, taking to heart the adage "Whoever gives something to another, he should do it in good faith." Marcus Cato presided over the case and rendered judgment.[205] This was the father of our own Cato. (We note here in passing that many people inherit a distinguished name from their fathers; but in this instance, he who produced such a shining figure in his progeny, must have his name known to history chiefly by reason of his son's fame). The judge issued the following ruling: "Since the seller was aware of this material issue when he sold the property, but did not disclose it, he ought to compensate the buyer for his loss."

---

[204] Augurs were religious officials who made predictions and performed divinations on the basis of their observations of birds in flight.

[205] This Cato was neither the Elder nor the Younger. He was a tribune of the plebs, the father of Cato the Younger and the grandson of Cato the Elder.

[67] So this was how he established a guideline for good faith. A defect known to the seller, he believed, should be disclosed to the buyer. If he has judged rightly, the grain merchant we spoke of earlier and the seller of the pest-ridden house were wrong to conceal material facts. The civil law cannot possibly anticipate all scenarios involving concealment; but those which it does anticipate are efficiently adjudicated.

Marcus Marius Gratidianus, a relative of ours, sold some property to Caius Sergio Orata.[206] He had actually bought the property a few years earlier from Orata himself. An easement existed on the property, but Marius had remained silent about this when drafting the purchase agreement. Orata retained Crassus as legal counsel and Gratidianus hired Antonius. Crassus argued for application of the law holding that "when a vendor knowingly fails to disclose defects, he ought to make the other party whole." Antonius based his arguments on fundamental fairness. "Because this defect had not been unknown to Sergio (as it was the same property Sergio previously sold to Marius), it had not been necessary to remind Sergio about it during the sale. He had not been deceived. For the man who had bought it (Sergio) already knew about the legal covenants that went with the land.

[68] What conclusion can we draw from these examples? That our ancestors did not take kindly to deceptive business ethics.

XVII. The law prohibits wily practices in one way, and philosophy prohibits them in another way. The law controls them through the reach of its power; and philosophers bring to bear reason and intellect. Reason mandates that our conduct be free from deviousness, defalcation and conscious misrepresentation. Does not deception exist in the very planning of a trap for the unwary, even if you never actually lure anyone into it, or you

---

[206] Caius Sergio Orata was praetor in 97 B.C. He got the name "Orata" supposedly from his fondness for either gold rings or goldfish.

never take a substantial step toward such a goal? To be sure, wild animals often fall into traps without any external impetus. If someone lists a house for sale, draws up the necessary documents, and then sells it despite its undisclosed defects, is not this person laying a trap for the unwary buyer?

[69] Because of the generally low level of popular culture, such ruthless practices are often not considered morally corrupt or may not even be explicitly banned by judicial law or civil codes; nevertheless, they are always frowned on by natural law. Society, indeed, has a reach that extends as far as those things that all men have in common. This has often been said, yet nevertheless must be declared more often. This concomitance is more intimate among people of the same ethnic group and closer among those who are citizens of the same state. It was for this reason that our ancestors preferred that there should be one concept of civil law and another concept of the "law of nations."[207]

The civil law may not necessarily be consistent with the law of nations; but the law of nations ought to be contained within the civil law. But in fact we have no unalloyed and pure models of Justice and Ideal Law; rather, we make use of shadows and images of these ideals.[208] If only we scrupulously followed even these! For they come from the best paradigms that Nature and Divine Truth have to offer.

[70] Be mindful of the importance of this saying: "Let me not be enticed or defrauded by you, or by my reliance on you." And these words, which are like gold: "Among the good there ought to be only good deeds, without even the whiff of fraud." But who are

---

[207] The distinctions here are *ius civile* (civil law) and the *ius gentium* ("law of nations" or universal law), which was the customary law that all nations or tribal groups might have in common. It can be thought of as a forerunner to international law.

[208] A statement laden with Platonic meaning. There are "ideal" versions of justice and law.

"the good," and what are "good deeds"? These are, to be sure, the key questions.

Indeed, Quintus Scaevola, the pontifex maximus, used to say that the phrase "in good faith" was of the greatest importance in every litigated matter. He believed that the phrase had nearly universal relevance, for it embraced guardianships, corporations, fiduciary relationships, commissions, vendor-buyer commercial codes, and labor and employment relations. In fact, it was applicable to nearly every dealing that might sustain a healthy society. A sharp legal mind was required to decide what duty was owed to whom and finally what legal opinion should be issued, since in most of these cases there would be opposing arguments of obvious merit.

[71] For this reason, chicanery and bad-faith dealings must be completely absent from our personal and commercial relations. These things like to masquerade as "wisdom," but in fact are completely different from it. Wisdom finds its role in the discernment of good and bad; and since everything that is morally corrupt is evil, bad faith elevates malice over goodwill.[209] The civil law, drawing from its sources in Nature, punishes bad faith and fraud not just in real estate transactions; it also forbids any kind of fraud on the part of the seller in the purchase of slaves. By edict of the aediles, the seller is presumed to be informed of his slave's health, possible fugitive status and criminal record. It is different, of course, in situations where ownership has come through bequest or inheritance.

[72] It may be determined from this, then, that because natural law is the ultimate source of guidance, it is in accordance with

---

[209] The word "malice" here is *malitia* in the original, which has no precise equivalent in English. Broadly, it means the deliberate perversion of law: i.e., the act of using a valid legal right for the commission of a morally wrong purpose, or the use of chicanery to defeat a legal right.

Nature that no one should act in a way that preys on the ignorance of another. No greater obscenity in life can be found than when wickedness cloaks itself with the pretense of intelligence. For it is from this origin that most situations arise in which advantageousness seems to conflict with moral goodness. Is it not true that few people can be found who would abstain from a contemplated wrong against someone else, if such a wrong could be done with impunity and without anyone's knowledge?

XVIII. [73] Let us subject our ideas to the crucible of the real world, if we dare. Let us use examples which the common man would not immediately recognize as bad acts; for it serves no purpose here to discuss examples of murderers, poisoners, forgers of wills, burglars or embezzlers. These types of people need to be restrained not by the words and discourses of philosophers, but rather by handcuffs and prison bars. We will instead consider the deeds and conduct of men who normally are thought of as good.

A forged will, alleged to be that of a wealthy man named Lucius Minucius Basilus, was brought from Greece to Rome by several people. In order to obtain the will's bequest more easily, the bearers of the will named two respected public figures, Marcus Crassus and Quintus Hortensius, as co-beneficiaries.[210] Although Crassus and Hortensius suspected the will to be false, they knew that they had no culpability in the matter; and they were willing to look the other way, as long as they could profit from the crime of another.

What should we make of this example? Is their conduct correct, as long as they appear to the public to have clean hands? I do not believe that their conduct was morally good. I say this

---

[210] Quintus Hortensius Hortalus (114—50 B.C.) was an orator and politician. Cicero dedicated a lost philosophical treatise to him (*Hortensius*) that inspired St. Augustine.

even though I had great affection for one of these men when he was alive, and do not hate the other one now that he is deceased.[211]

[74] Basilus had wanted Marcus Satrius,[212] his sister's son, to bear his name and so made him an heir. (I am here referring to the man known as the patron of the Picenum and Sabine regions. And what a disgraceful sign of the times is this fact!) It was hardly fair that a couple of Rome's leading notables would inherit something, while Satrius would inherit nothing except a name. If a man neither safeguards another from injury, nor diverts injury when he can, then he is complicit in wrongdoing, as I explained in the first book of this treatise. If so, what must we then think of someone who not only *does not* try to divert harm, but is actually complicit in causing it? Frankly, it is my view that even valid inheritances are irredeemably tainted if they are secured through insincere blandishments or fake gestures.

We see in these kinds of examples how a thing can sometimes appear to be expedient and at other times appear morally good. *But this appearance is deceptive.* The basic principle remains the same whether we are talking about expediency or moral goodness.

[75] He who does not absorb this truth will never be free from the impulse to defraud or from the temptations of crime. If a man thinks to himself, "This way truly is the morally right path, but this other one is more advantageous," he is erroneously trying to separate two things that Nature has intended to be fused together. And this is the font from which flow the waters of crime, wicked deeds and other kinds of immoral behavior.

XIX. If a good man had the hypothetical power to insert his name into the wills of wealthy people with the snap of his fingers, he would not use this power even if no one would ever be able to

---

[211] The one Cicero "did not hate" was Crassus. The two were bitter rivals for a time, but eventually reconciled.

[212] Marcus Satrius was an associate of Antony and not liked by Cicero.

find out about it. But if you were to give such power to Marcus Crassus—that with a with a snap of his fingers he could be designated as heir to a will when he had no legal right to be one—I believe he would have danced for joy in the forum. A just man, someone whom we may truly call a good man, is one who would not take something for himself that he improperly acquired from someone else. Whoever is unnerved by this definition is someone who admits to not knowing what a good man really is.

[76] If anyone truly wanted to disclose his notion of a "good man" that is embedded in his own mind, he would explain that a good man is one who tries to assist others when he can and who harms no one unless attacked first. What more can be said? Would not a person be doing harm, if he used a magic potion to remove the lawful heirs of an estate from the picture, and in their place substituted himself?

Maybe someone will here say, "So shouldn't he do what is expedient and advantageous?" Our answer must be no. Anyone asking such a question must be made to understand that *nothing that is unjust can be either expedient or advantageous*. He who is unable to learn this is incapable of becoming a good man.

[77] When I was a boy, I once heard a story from my father about the consul Caius Fimbria.[213] Fimbria, as a judge, had presided over a case involving one Marcus Lutatius Pinthia, a knight of impeccable reputation. Pinthia bet the court that he could prove he was a "good man." But Fimbria told him that he would never issue a ruling on such a matter. He feared he might either deprive a man of his good name if he had to rule against him, or that he might be boxed into issuing a decree that a litigant was a "good man," when in fact the only way to acquire this title is to bear numerous responsibilities and earn praise for carrying them out.

---

[213] Caius Flavius Fimbria was an orator and jurist, and co-consul with Marius in 104 B.C.

Both Socrates and Fimbria knew that any "good man" worthy of the name would appreciate that something morally wrong can never be expedient. Such a man would not do something or even think of doing something that he would not have the courage to say openly beforehand. Is it not a disgrace when philosophers vacillate over things that the common man sees as self-evidently true?

The following adage is of folk origin and nearly worn out from overuse. When they want to praise someone's honesty and moral excellence, they say that one can "throw numbers at him in the dark."[214] This can have no other meaning than the following: what is morally wrong cannot be expedient, even if you can prevail without anyone being able to stop you.

[78] Hearing this proverb, do you see how we cannot excuse the conduct either of Gyges (whom we spoke of earlier), or of the hypothetical person who has the power to snap his fingers and acquire everyone's inheritances? What is morally wicked cannot, no matter how artfully it is concealed, be made into something morally good. And what is not morally good cannot be transformed into something advantageous. Nature despises the attempt, and recoils from it.

XX. [79] Indeed, the justifications for sinning are often heard when the rewards for doing so are great. Caius Marius had at one time lost all hope of attaining the consulship; it was seven years after he left the office of praetor and it was commonly believed he

---

[214] The phrase is *quicum in tenebris mices*, which literally means, "You may flash with him in the dark." According to the Oxford Latin Dictionary's entry for the verb *micare*, the "flashing" referred to was a number guessing-game called *morra*. One had to guess the total number of fingers "flashed" by the opponent. The point of the adage was to note that someone could be so honest that they would tell you the correct number of fingers thrown out, even if the lights were out and no one else could see them.

would never try to seek higher office. As an ambassador for Quintus Metellus, a great man and citizen, he was sent to Rome pursuant to Metellus's authority.

Before the Roman people, he actually accused Metellus of prolonging the war;[215] and he said that if they made him consul, he would in a short time deliver Jugurtha dead or alive into Roman hands. He was indeed made consul; but he had abandoned all sense of personal integrity and honor. Through false accusations he caused a good and distinguished citizen, whom he was supposed to be representing, to be smeared with calumny and lies.

[80] Even our own Gratidianus did not perform as is expected of a good man when he was in office. When he was praetor, the tribunes of the people convened the college of praetors in order to issue a decree on fiscal policy. The currency at that time was so volatile that no one knew exactly how to determine the fair market value of his assets. They jointly drafted an edict and proposed sanctions and penalties for its violation; and it was agreed that they would ascend the rostra as a group in the afternoon.[216] Some departed one way and others another way. But Marius,[217] even though it had been agreed that the edict would be published jointly, went directly from the benches in the assembly hall to the rostra and publicly proclaimed the edict alone. And this little stunt, if you ask me, brought him great notoriety. Statues of him appeared in every neighborhood and before these were placed frankincense and candles. What more can I say? No one was ever more loved by the crowd.

[81] These, then, are the types of situations that sometimes can put our consciences to the test: I am talking about cases where

---

[215] I.e., the Jugurthine War, 112-106 B.C. Quintus Metellus was consul in 109 B.C. and assumed the prosecution of the war.

[216] Edicts and ordinances would be publicly announced from the rostra.

[217] Gratidianus.

justice is not greatly violated, but *the results* of such a violation are very great. For Marius[218] to snatch away public credit from his colleagues and the tribunes was not in itself deeply evil. But to use this bit of demagoguery to gain the consulship, which he had disclosed as his goal, was exceedingly opportunistic.

Know that there is one basic principle above all others that I wish you to retain: *what seems advantageous must not be morally wrong, and what is morally wrong must not be considered advantageous.* What can we conclude from this? Can we consider Caius Marius or Marius Gratidianus to be good men? Search through and use your own intelligence as you see fit to identify what qualities of a "good man" they might possess. Do lying, spreading calumnies for one's own benefit, stealing or deceiving comport with the idea of being a good man? Absolutely not, of course.

[82] Is there anything of such value or so worth seeking that you would be willing to lose your good name, or forfeit the privilege of being known as a good man? What exactly is it that this "expediency" can give us that might even begin to balance out what is lost when we throw away our sense of trust, justice, and our claim to be a good man? Is there really any difference whether a man changes himself completely into a beast or if he simply bears the external image of a man while remaining a beast behind this mask?

XXI. What else? Isn't it true that those who ignore what is right and honest in order to chase after power behave in the same way as the groom who wants to have a father-in-law that will help him gain influence?[219] He thought what he did was the most advantageous thing possible, and at the same time, that all the

---

[218] This again refers to Gratidianus (see note 106).
[219] Reference to Pompey.

200

negative consequences could be shifted to someone else. He could not see how unjust and how morally wrong his schemes were to his country. The same father-in-law[220] always used to repeat some lines of Greek verse from *The Phoenician Women*,[221] which I will reproduce in a general way as far as I can remember:

> If the law must be violated, it must be violated for the sake of the ruler;
> You can cultivate your piety with other things.

When he brought about the one thing that was the most heinous crime of all, the death penalty was the result.[222]

[83] Why do we offer up this information here about fraudulent buying, selling, and inheritances? Remember that there was a man who wanted to be the king of the Roman people and lord of the whole world and he accomplished this goal.[223] He who says that this was a morally sound objective has a warped mind. He approves of the repression of law and personal liberties and thinks that the foul and detestable quashing of these things is beautiful. He who recognizes that this act was not morally right for our country, which was formerly free and should be free now, and who thinks that it is expedient for someone to achieve absolute power, then what protest or pleading can I really use to pull him away from such an error? Immortal gods! Can the most foul and disgraceful strangling of one's own country ever be

---

[220] Caesar became Pompey's father-in-law (*socer*) after Pompey married Caesar's daughter Julia in 59 B.C.

[221] A play by Euripides, also called the *Phoenissae*. The lines quoted here are spoken by the character Eteocles (V.534). Seneca also composed a play with the same title.

[222] I.e., Caesar's assassination was justified due to his supposed desire to become king and abolish the republic.

[223] Reference to Caesar.

considered expedient, even when the person who has subjugated his fellow citizens is honored with the title of "father of his country"?[224]

Expediency, therefore, must be aligned with morality. And even if there be a difference between these two words, let them seem to sound as one.[225]

[84] I have no response to the view of the rabble that there is nothing more advantageous than to be a ruler. Yet when I begin to examine things from the perspective of absolute truth, I find that nothing could be less advantageous than if someone were to attain a goal through deliberate injustice. Can mental anxieties, unrelenting stress, days and nights of fear, and a life packed with dangers and plots ever be "advantageous" to anyone? As Accius says,

> Many connivers and schemers are drawn to the monarch, but few well-wishers.[226]

But whose court was Accius referring to? The one that was obtained by Tantalus and bequeathed lawfully to Penelope. Now, how many more "connivers and schemers" do you think that our own "monarch" had, who oppressed the Roman people with its own military forces and forced a state—which was not only free but had justly administered other nations—to service his own personal needs?[227]

---

[224] Caesar was given the title of *parens patriae* ("father of his country") in 45 B.C. It galled Cicero that this was the same title that he himself had been given for saving the republic from the conspiracy of Catiline some years earlier.

[225] *Et quidem sic, ut haec duo verbo inter se discrepare, re unum sonare videantur.*

[226] Lucius Accius (or Lucius Attius) was a Roman tragic poet (c.170—86 B.C.). He wrote about fifty plays, but only fragments of his work survive.

[227] Another reference to Caesar and his supposed desire to become king.

[85] What blemishes do you think he had on his conscience, what wounds on his spirit? And whose life can be considered "advantageous" if it is lived under the condition that whoever extinguishes that life will receive the greatest thanks and glory? These things we have been discussing, which may seem to be expedient, are clearly not so, since closer inspection shows them to be full of vice and wickedness. We ought to be sufficiently persuaded, then, that nothing is advantageous that is not morally right.

XXII. [86] Although this principle has been illustrated often in history, it was declared compellingly by Caius Fabricius in the war against Pyrrhus during his second consulship and by our own senate. When King Pyrrhus wantonly launched a war against the Roman people, it became for us a major power struggle against a capable and well-connected foreign sovereign. One of Pyrrhus's deserters came into Fabricius's camp and promised the consul— if he could obtain a reward—that he could sneak back into Pyrrhus's camp and clandestinely bring about his death through poisoning. Fabricius took care that this man was turned over to Pyrrhus; and the senate commended Fabricius for this action. If we were seeking the outward show of expediency and its superficial benefits, we might have been tempted by this one deserter, who could have ended a great war and a major challenge to our power. Yet it would have been a great dishonor and shame to have overcome such a foe by a criminal act, rather than through the exercise of martial virtue.

[87] Which choice was more expedient for Fabricius (who was for our city what Aristides was for Athens) or for our senate, who both never disconnected advantageousness from human dignity, when presented with the option of confronting a foe with arms or with poison? If empire is sought for glory's sake, the quest should be free of criminality; for there is no glory in evil. But if power itself is pursued by any means possible, it can never be advantageous if it is gained through foul means.

For example, a proposal of Lucius Philippus, the son of Quintus, was certainly not advantageous. The dictator Lucius Sulla, having accepted sums of money from certain city-states, waived certain of their financial obligations with the consent of the senate. Philippus insisted that we[228] return these states to their former status as taxable entities without regard for the money that they had already paid for their tax-exempt status. And the senate was in agreement with him. What a disgusting exercise of power! There is more good faith among pirates than in the senate. As the saying goes, "As the tax revenues grow, so does expediency." How long will people have the nerve to say that what is morally rotten can be expedient?

[88] Indeed, how can hatred and infamy ever be advantageous for any authority, when true authority ought instead to be bolstered by legitimate prestige and the goodwill of allies? I have often differed from my friend Cato on this issue. He seemed to me to be too stern in his monitoring of the treasury and his insistence on tax revenues. He denied much to the tax farmers,[229] and much to our allies, at a time when we ought to have been more generous with them. They should have been dealt with in the same way as our tenants, probably even better, since mutual trust between our social orders was essential to the health of our republic. Curio was also misguided when he used to say that the people beyond the Po

---

[228] I.e., the senate.

[229] The word I have rendered as "tax farmer" is *publicanus*, which means a "contractor for the collection of taxes or dues," according to the Oxford Latin Dictionary. A "tax farmer" or "publican" usually belonged to the equestrian class. He functioned as a contractor responsible for the completion of public works projects and the collection of tax revenues. They would have to bid on large projects from the senate, where there could be risks of insider dealings, conflicts of interest, and abuse. A group of tax farmers asked the senate for tax relief, but Cato opposed it. As Cicero notes, Cato's inflexible attitude did much to drive them into Caesar's camp.

had valid political grievances, but then would tack on this statement: "Let expediency win!"[230] It would have been better to demonstrate that the grievances were not valid, because they were not advantageous for the republic, than to acknowledge that they were just, when he said that they were not advantageous.

XXIII. [89] The sixth book of Hecaton's treatise *On Duties* is full of these sorts of questions: "whether it is right for a good man not to feed his domestic servants when food is at a very high price." He discusses both sides of the issue, but in the end, he believes that such moral questions should be determined by letting expediency, rather than humanitarianism, have the last word.

He also asks this question: if a ship's crew must throw some of its cargo into the sea,[231] should it sacrifice an expensive horse or a worthless slave? Concerns for property lead him one way, and his conscience another way.

"What if an idiot floating in the water has found a piece of wood from a shipwreck. Should a wise man be able to take it away from him, if he can?" Hecaton says no, since that would be unjust.

"And should the owner of the ship be permitted to take the wood from the idiot?"

"Certainly not, no more than if the ship were on the high seas, the owner should be allowed to throw someone overboard just because he claimed the ship was his. For until a ship has reached the destination that was the advertised purpose of the voyage, the ship belongs to those making the journey, not to the owner."

[90] "And what about this? What if there is only one piece of timber, and two men flailing in the ocean, both of them wise men? Should they both take it jointly, or should one give way for the other?"

---

[230] Caius Scribonius Curio. There was a father and son with this name, but this likely refers to the son, who died in 53 B.C.
[231] To lighten its load.

"Certainly one should make way for the other. But if it is to be so, it should be the one whose life is worth more, either intrinsically, or as it seems in the eyes of his country.

"But what if both men are of equal worth?"

"There would be no fight between them. It would be decided by lot, or by a game of *morra*,[232] or if one would give his place to the other."

"What about this? If a father were robbing temples or digging a tunnel to break into the treasury, should his son tell the authorities on him?"

"That would be a violation of divine law. The son should defend the father, if he were charged with the crime."

"But doesn't one's country come first, before any other duties?"

"Yes, very much so. But it is the best thing for our country to have citizens who believe in filial piety."

"And what if the father tried to seize power as a tyrant and tried to act arbitrarily with his country, should his son then stand silent?"

"The son would try to plead with his father and beg him not to take this course. If this doesn't work, he may reprimand him and then warn him sternly. In extreme cases, if he sees things headed towards the nation's ruin, he will place the welfare of his country before the welfare of his father."

[91] The hypothetical questioner asks again: "If a wise man unsuspectingly accepts counterfeit currency for some goods, and later discovers its falsity, will he then use this money to settle a debt with someone else?" Diogenes says this is permitted. Antipater says it is not, and I concur.

---

[232] The number guessing game described previously, represented by the verb *micare*. Players extend their hands out, revealing fingers, and the object is the guess the total number.

Should a man who knowingly sells wine about to go sour disclose this fact about his product? Diogenes says this is not necessary but Antipater believes it to be good man's obligation. These questions resemble the legal controversies of the Stoics.

"In selling a slave, should someone disclose not only those defects that, unless disclosed, would require the slave's return under the civil law, but also non-mandatory information, such as the fact that the slave is crafty, a gambler, a thief or has a taste for alcohol?" One authority believes such disclosures should be made and the other does not.

[92] "And if a man selling gold believes he is actually selling brass, should a good man let him know this? Or should he buy for one *denarius* what should really cost a thousand *denarii*?" It can be seen from the examples above what my own views are. It is also clear what the opposing views are of the other thinkers I have named.

XXIV. Agreements and promises must always be kept, as long as they are made "neither through coercion nor bad faith," as the praetors are accustomed to say in their rulings. Suppose one man gives another some medicine for the treatment of skin edema with the condition that he use the medicine once only, and then never again. Suppose further that the man is cured of his condition, but later contracts the same affliction, and he is unable to get permission from the original medicine donor to use it again. What should be done? Since anyone denying such permission would be inhuman, and since his using the medicine would not harm anyone, the sick man must do what is necessary for his own life and health.

[93] And for another example? Imagine if a wise man were told by someone willing to leave him an inheritance of a hundred million sesterces that he must dance in public view in the forum as a condition of receiving the money. Suppose he promised to do this, because he knew that otherwise he would not be written into the will. Is this the right thing to do, or not? I wish he had not

made this promise; I think it clearly was undignified. But he has made the promise. If he considers dancing publicly in the forum to be morally wrong, it would be better that he take nothing from the inheritance than if he took something, unless perhaps he chooses to donate the money to the state treasury for some critical use. On the other hand, he may see nothing immoral about dancing for money in the forum, when done for the pecuniary benefit of one's country.

XXV. [94] Those promises which are not expedient to those whom you give them, also do not need to be kept. If we may revisit an old fable, we may recall that the god Sol made a promise to his son Phaethon that he would do whatever the son wished. The son asked to be taken on his father's chariot and this was granted. Before the ride ended he was struck by a bolt of lightning. How much better would it have been if the father had not fulfilled his promise![233]

And what about that promise that Theseus secured from Neptune? When Neptune gave him three wishes, Theseus wished for the death of his son Hippolytus, because he suspected there was something going on between the son and his stepmother. But when this wish was granted, Theseus became crippled with the greatest sorrow.

[95] When Agamemnon promised to the goddess Diana the most beautiful youth born in his kingdom in a certain year, he sacrificed Iphegenia, since no child born that year was more beautiful than she. Rather than carry out such a terrible pledge, it would have been better not to make such a vow in the first place. Therefore, promises sometimes need not be kept and deposits need not always be returned. If a man places his sword in your

---

[233] See Ovid, *Metam.* II.325. But at least Phaethon tried. Ovid gives him a nice epitaph: *Hic situs est Phaethon, currus auriga paterni quem si non tenuit magnis tamen excidit ausis.* Which means, "Here lies Phaethon. Driver of his father's chariot, he could not hold it, but he still failed with great daring."

custody when he is of sound mind and asks for it back when he is boiling with rage, it would be unconscionable to give it back. In fact, it would be your duty not to do so.

If someone deposits a sum of money with you in trust and then plans to carry out violent acts against your country, do you give him back his money? I believe not. Your doing so would be an act against your nation; and your nation is something that should be most precious to you. Clearly, there are many things that seem by nature to be morally good, but which under certain circumstances are not so.

The making of a promise, the honoring of a covenant, and the restoring of funds held in trust, may all become *not* morally good, depending on the expediency of the external circumstances. I believe I have now said enough about those things which seem to be expedient, but which, wearing the false mask of prudence, are in fact contrary to justice.

[96] Since in book one we described how duties come from the four kinds of moral goodness,[234] let us apply this same blueprint in pointing out those things that *seem* to be expedient but are in fact harmful to virtue. We have already discussed wisdom, which wickedness loves to imitate, and we have described justice, which always is expedient. It remains for us to describe the two divisions of moral goodness. One of these divisions is to be found in a soul of great grandeur and surpassing excellence; the other division is to be found in the shaping and polishing of this soul through the disciplines of continence and temperance.

XXVI. [97] The following subterfuge seemed expedient to Ulysses, at least according to how the tragic poets have portrayed him.[235] In Homer's view (our most reliable authority), he was

---

[234] I.e., the classifications laid out in book one.
[235] Tragic poets would include also the dramatists Euripides, Aeschylus and Sophocles.

beyond suspicion. But the dramatic tragedies accuse Ulysses of wanting to evade military service by the ruse of feigning insanity. It was not an honorable course of action, but an expedient one, as someone might possibly say.

"To play the role of lord and to live a life of leisure in Ithaca with his parents, wife and son: who would not want this? Do you think there is any glory in daily labors and dangers, when compared to this kind of domestic tranquility?"

But for my part, I would condemn and reject this shirking of one's obligations. I say this because I believe that what is not morally good is also not expedient.

[98] What do you think Ulysses would have heard from other people, if he had continued to feign insanity? This was the man who was such a credit to his army in war. And yet he had to listen to these words from Ajax:

> He himself first swore the oath, and you all know this,
> And it was he alone who broke trust:
> He continued to feign madness, that he might avoid battle.
> He might have continued to deceive, despite his binding and
> Sacred vow, had not the canny and observant Palamedes
> Sniffed out his crafty effrontery.[236]

[99] It was better for Ulysses to fight—not only with the enemy, but also with the open sea—than it was to abandon the united Greeks when they were engaged in a war with barbarians.

---

[236] These lines are likely from something written either by Accius (c.170—86 B.C.) or Marcus Pacuvius (c.220—130 B.C.). The latter was a renowned tragic poet who survives only in fragments. According to legend, the Palamedes referred to here was the son of Nauplius, king of Euboea. Ulysses pretended to be insane while plowing a field. To test him, Palamedes placed a young child in front of the plow. Ulysses had no choice but to stop, thereby demonstrating his sanity.

But let us set aside ancient fables and foreign events and turn our attention to the historical record in our own country. Marcus Atilius Regulus, when he was consul for a second time in Africa, had been captured in an ambush by the Spartan Xanthippus, who was himself serving under the general Hamilcar, the father of Hannibal.[237] Regulus was sent to the Roman senate to negotiate an arrangement whereby certain Carthaginian nobles imprisoned there might be freed. Unless he was successful, he was sworn to return to captivity in Carthage.

When he arrived in Rome, he saw the apparent advantage of expediency; but he judged this to be an illusion, as events would show. This was his option: to remain in his country, to be at home with his wife and children, and to accept the disaster that had happened to him in war. The military debacle would have been judged simply as part of the routine fortunes of war and he might have continued to hold his position of consular dignity.

Who would deny that this option appeared advantageous? Whom do you think? Greatness of soul and personal valor would deny it.

XXVII. [100] Do you need a more well-placed example of the ideas we are talking about? It is typical of the nobler virtues to fear nothing, to look down on all petty human conduct, and to believe that nothing that happens to a man can be intolerable.

But what did he do? He came to the senate, explained his mandate from the Carthaginians, and recused himself from

---

[237] Regulus was captured in battle during his second consulship at the Battle of Bagradas (also called the Battle of Tunis) in 255 B.C. About 12,000 Romans were slain, and about 5,000 captured. This event actually occurred in the year *after* Regulus's second consulship. In addition, the Hamilcar whom Cicero refers to was not Hamilcar Barca, the father of Hannibal. The two are often confused. Very little is known of the Hamilcar referred to here by Cicero, except that he enjoyed successes at the battles of Drepanum and Thermae in the First Punic War.

casting a vote on the issue; he said that as long as he was bound by the oath made to the enemy, he was not a senator. (Of course someone will here say, "What a stupid man! How could he work against his own advantage?") He further said that it was not expedient for Rome that the Carthaginian captives be sent back home. The prisoners were young men and vigorous leaders, while he himself was advanced in age.

And when his way of thinking prevailed, the prisoners were kept in Rome, while he returned to Carthage. Neither his longing for his native land, nor the desire to be with his family could keep him at Rome. And neither was he unmindful of the fact that he was heading back to a most cruel enemy, and a set of exquisite tortures. Keeping his word was the primary object in his mind. So when he was being slowly executed through sleep deprivation, it was still a better fate than if he had puttered around in Rome as an old, broken captive, a consul unworthy of the name.

[101] You may think that it was stupid for someone not only to suggest that the captives not be returned, but also to advocate strongly against it. But how was this decision foolish? Was it not done for the benefit of the republic? And is it possible that something which is disadvantageous to the state be advantageous for a private citizen?

XXVIII. Men corrupt the foundational principles of Nature when they separate expediency from moral goodness. Indeed, we all seek out expediency and are carried towards it; we cannot really behave in any other way. Where can we find a man who runs away from expediency? Or who, stated another way, does not pursue expediency zealously? But because we can nowhere find true expediencies except in merit, virtue and moral goodness, we should for this reason have these things as our primary and unshakeable principles; and we should consider the term "expediency" not as a decorative showpiece, but as a vital requirement for life.

[102] Someone will ask: "But for what purpose, then, is an

oath?" Do we fear an angry Jove? It is the common view of all philosophers—not just the view of those who say that God does not fret about minor nuisances and dwell on trifles, but also the view of those who prefer to see God planning and directing the universe—that God is not affected by "anger" and does not go out of his way to hurt mankind. How could Jupiter have possibly harmed Regulus more than he harmed himself? Religion had no such power that could subvert this kind of expediency.

Or was Regulus acting wrongly? The least of several evils is the best choice. Did a moral disgrace involve as much evil as that torture he suffered? Finally, consider these words from Accius:

> *Thyestes*: Have you broken faith?
> *Atreus*: I have neither given, nor do I give, trust to the unfaithful.[238]

Although this statement is mouthed by a corrupt king, it is still said with a truth that resonates deeply.

[103] The skeptics again advance the following objection: "In the same way that we believe some things are expedient but are not, so we believe some things to be morally right that are not. It *appeared* to be morally good for Regulus to return to captivity and torture for the sake of preserving his oath to Carthage. But this was *not* morally right: because his promise was extracted under duress, it ought not to have been valid." The doubters also say this: "Whatever truly is expedient may at some point become morally good, even though it may not have been so previously." These are the objections raised against Regulus's decision. We will discuss them here in order.

XXIX. [104] Someone here might say, "He did not need to fear that an enraged Jupiter would hurt him; the god is not in the

---

[238] The gist of the saying is that one may break one's word to a treacherous party.

habit of being angry or inflicting harm." This reasoning, indeed, is worth no more when applied to Regulus's decision than it is when applied to all types of oaths in general. *With regard to oaths, one should be preoccupied not by the fear of breaking it, but rather by the oath's underlying purpose.* In fact, an oath may be considered an affirmation with religious underpinnings. The act of making a promise must be seen, then, as a sort of testimony before God. What is relevant in this process is not the "anger of the gods" (since this does not exist), but adherence to justice and fidelity. Ennius summarized these things well when he said:

> O nourishing Faith, fitted with lofty wings, and the sacred oath of Jove![239]

So when someone violates his word, he violates Faith herself. Our ancestors wanted this same spirit to permeate the capitol, as we can see in one of Cato's speeches when he called Faith the "neighbor of Jupiter, best and brightest."

[105] But would perhaps an enraged Jupiter not have harmed Regulus more than Regulus hurt himself? Certainly, if we believe that there is no evil except to feel pain. But in fact, it is not only *not* the worst evil, but it is no evil at all, as the most important philosophers assure us. I ask that you not find fault with Regulus by seeing him as a trivial example; I do not know a more serious case than that of Regulus. What more substantial exemplar can we ask for than that of one of the most notable Roman citizens, who voluntarily submitted himself to torture for the sake of adhering to a moral purpose?

Our skeptics will here interject: "Select the least of a group of evils." By this they mean that a moral failing is preferable to a physical disaster. But is there any greater evil than moral

---

[239] Probably from his *Thyestes*.

corruption? If the sight of physical deformity generates some offense in others, how much aversion and vileness can be seen in a human soul that is rotted with moral corruption?

[106] For this reason, those who probe deeply into these issues have the courage to say that *the only evil is what is morally corrupt.* Even those who are more casual about this sort of thing do not shy away from calling it the greatest evil. Indeed, these words are most appropriate here:

I have neither given, nor do I give, anything to the unfaithful.

These words from the poet ring true, because when the character of Atreus was being worked out, he must have been mindful of all the details of his persona. But if people intend to employ this as a general rule (that an oath given to the faithless is not a true oath), let them take care that they are not actually engaging in a subterfuge that has perjury as its goal.

[107] The law of warfare must, however, be preserved; and so must fidelity to an oath given to an enemy. What has been promised by oath with a mind fully informed and prepared to honor the promise, must be done. But otherwise, if there is no such "meeting of the minds," then there is no breach of the oath if the promise is not fulfilled.

For example, if an agreement is made with pirates regarding a ransom for a captive, and you do not deliver the money, there is no fraud, even if you do not perform as you have promised. For a pirate is not counted as a recognized foreign national enemy. He is the antagonist of the entire world. We owe him neither faithfulness to our promises nor any binding covenant.

[108] To swear an oath falsely is not always perjury. But when you swear to a sentiment that "truly comes from the mind" (as we employ these words in our legal customs), then it becomes perjury if you do not follow through. Recall the words of Euripides:

I have made the oath with my tongue, but my mind remains unsworn.[240]

Regulus ought not to have disturbed with perjury the wartime terms and agreements with the enemy. The war was being waged with legitimacy and legality against a national foe; and in pursuit of this purpose, we have our whole body of fetial law,[241] as well as many international laws. If this were not so, our senate would never have turned over such great men in chains to the other side.

XXX. [109] When Titus Veturius and Spurius Postumius were serving their second terms as consuls, they made peace with the Samnites after the battle at the Caudine Forks went badly. Our legions were then sent under the yoke.[242] The two generals were given to the enemy, as they had concluded peace without the direction of the senate and Roman people. At the same time, and in order to repudiate the peace with the Samnites, Tiberius Numicius and Quintus Maelius, the tribunes of the people, were also given over to the enemy. This was because peace had been concluded with their authority. And Postumius, who had been turned over because of his surrender, was the initiator and advocate of this policy.

---

[240] From *Hippolytus* 613.

[241] The fetial law (*ius fetiale*) refers to the war-declaring functions of the Roman fetials. The fetials were a type of priest, who together (as part of a college) advised the senate on matters of international law and war. Livy describes them in I.24 and I.32.

[242] The Battle of the Caudine Forks took place in 321 B.C. during the Second Samnite War. No blood was shed; the Romans were trapped by the Samnites and surrendered. To "send under the yoke" (*sub iugum mittere*) was an ancient ritual given to defeated forces in battle. The vanquished were made to walk under the raised spears of the victors. Originally meant as a way ceremonially to purge the guilt of the fallen, it developed into an effective way to drive home the lesson that one was defeated.

The same thing happened a few years after this, when Caius Mancinus had concluded a treaty with the Numantines without the senate's authority.[243] He then recommended that he himself be given over to the enemy and this measure was carried in the senate by Lucius Furius and Sextus Atilius. When the measure passed the senate, he was turned over. His action was more morally correct than that of Quintus Pompeius; although Pompeius's situation was the same as his, the bill did not pass because of his political lobbying against it.[244] We can see in this example that expediency got the better of moral goodness. In the earlier examples we have discussed, the false appearance of expediency was overcome by the authority of moral rectitude.

[110] Someone here might say, "He ought not to have honored his promise, as it was extracted under duress." As if force could actually be effective against a brave man! Why, then, did he go to the senate, when he would have advised against releasing the war captives? If you find fault with this, then you find fault with the greatest feature of his conduct. He did not base his actions on his own judgment; he took up the case in order that it might be the senate's judgment. Had he not been the originator of the proposal, the captives might have been sent back to the Carthaginians. Regulus might have stayed in his country and remained alive. But he did not believe this was advantageous for his country and felt it was morally right to act another way. And he was fully prepared to suffer for it.

---

[243] Caius Hostilius Mancinus in 137 B.C. had control of the war against Numantia in Spain.

[244] As consul in 141 B.C., Quintus Pompeius was sent to Spain to continue the Numantine War. He made peace with the Numantines when things started to go badly for him. His conduct was later discovered by his replacement. At senate hearings on the matter, Pompeius denied wrongdoing, and escaped punishment. He seemed to have led a charmed life, for he also prevailed in an unrelated accusation against him for extortion.

When they say that what is powerfully expedient can "become" morally good, it is much better to say that something *is* morally good, not that it *may become* morally good. There is nothing expedient that is not morally good. Neither can something be morally good just because it happens to be expedient. When something is expedient, it is so because it is morally good. We conclude that, from the many amazing examples in history, one would hardly be able to find an example more deserving of praise or admiration than that of Regulus.

XXXI. [111] Out of all of Regulus's meritorious actions, the one most worthy of admiration was when he recommended the retention of the prisoners of war. It seems almost unbelievable to us now that he would have returned to Carthage, but in those days it would not have been possible to do otherwise. Such glory does not belong to the man, but to his era. For our ancestors wished no bond holding together mutual trust to be as sacred as that provided by a solemn oath. The laws of the Twelve Tables reveal this.[245] The existence of the *sacratae* reveals this.[246] Official treaties also reveal this, where good faith is owed even to the enemy. It is also revealed by the judicial examinations and penalties levied by the censors; they judged nothing more scrupulously than cases involving formal oaths.

[112] Lucius Manlius (the son of Aulus), when he was acting

---

[245] The Laws of the Twelve Tables, formally promulgated in 449 B.C., were one of the cornerstones of Roman law. Livy (III.57) says they were inscribed in bronze and publicly posted.

[246] This term has no precise equivalent in English except the rendering of "sacred laws." A sacred law (*lex sacrata*) had religious overtones, going back to the prehistoric customs of taboos. A sacred law was one which, when broken, placed a curse on the violator, his family and his property. Such laws were used to protect religious property (such as temples) or sacrosanct persons (such as Vestal Virgins). The idea was that a violator was offending the gods as well as mortals.

as dictator, was accused by a tribune of the people named Marcus Pomponius of improperly adding a few days to his term of office.[247] Pomponius also indicted him for placing his son Titus (who later added the name Torquatus) under house arrest and banishing him to a rural area. When the young son learned of these political problems, we are told that he traveled to Rome and, at the first light of day, visited the private home of Pomponius. Once the angry visitor was announced to Pomponius, he rose from his bed, asked all present to leave and ordered the son to be brought to him; he believed that some new issues in the case would be brought to his attention.

When Titus confronted Pomponius, he suddenly drew a short sword from his robe and swore that he would kill the tribune unless he dismissed the case against his father. Overcome with fear, Pomponius gave his word that he would do this. He made a public report on this case, and explained why it was necessary to dismiss the indictment against Manlius. This was what an oath was worth in those days.

The boy of this story was the same Titus Manlius who killed a Gaul that had challenged him to combat during the Battle of the Anio.[248] His surname (Torquatus) came from the fact that he removed the Gaul's torque.[249] During his third consulship,[250] he routed the Latins and put them to flight in a battle along the Veseris. He was one of the greatest of the great; and while he was very indulgent towards his father, he was incredibly severe in his dealings with his son.[251]

---

[247] Lucius Manlius Capitolinus was dictator in 363 B.C.

[248] An event that occurred in 361 B.C. when Titus Manlius was fighting in the army of Titus Quinctius Poenus against the Gauls.

[249] A torque (also spelled torc or torq) was an ornamental neck ring made either from braided metal or from a single piece of metal. They were worn by Scythian, Gallic and Illyrian peoples.

[250] In 340 B.C.

[251] So said because he is supposed to have ordered the execution of his son for a breach of discipline.

XXXII. [113] Just as the worthy Regulus is noted for how he kept his word, so the ten Roman prisoners sworn to their word whom Hannibal sent to the senate after the Battle of Cannae deserve to be condemned. They had given Hannibal their word that they would return to the camp (captured by the Carthaginians) if they could not obtain the release of some of the enemy's prisoners of war.

Among historians there is no general consensus on the details of what happened. Polybius, one of the very best authorities, says that of the ten nobles sent on the negotiation mission, nine returned to Hannibal once their efforts failed.[252] One of the ten, who a little while earlier had left the Carthaginian camp and then gone back under the pretext of having forgotten something there, remained in Rome. He tried to claim that his "going back" to the camp freed him from his obligation to honor the oath made to Hannibal. This was untrue. Fraud only makes perjury worse; it does not wash it away. He displayed a perverse and foolish deviousness that camouflaged itself as prudence; it was for this reason that the senate ordered the cunning schemer to be led back to Hannibal in chains.

[114] But this is the most important point: Hannibal held eight thousand prisoners of war. These were not men he had captured on the battlefield or ones that who had fled in fear for their lives during combat. Rather, they were men who had been left at camp by the consuls Paulus and Varro.[253] The senate decided not to pay a ransom for these captives; even though it would have cost little money, it was believed to be better to send our soldiers the

---

[252] Polybius VI.56.

[253] The Roman commanders during the Battle of Cannae (216 B.C.) were the consuls Caius Terentius Varro and Lucius Aemilius Paullus. The famous battle at Cannae, of course, was one of the great disasters in Roman history, and Hannibal's supreme military achievement.

message that they should either be victorious or die fighting. Hannibal, having heard this news, became truly demoralized; for although Rome had suffered a huge disaster, the senate and the people still retained their fighting spirit. Thus, when we compare these options, what appears to be expedient is eclipsed by what is morally correct.

[115] Caius Acilius,[254] the author of a work of history in Greek, tells us that there were many who played this same game of fraudulently returning to camp, in order to create a pretext for breaking their oaths. They were marked out for every public humiliation by the Roman censors.

Let us move on from this matter. From our discussion it is clear that things done with a timid, abject, broken and wavering spirit, as the action of Regulus would have been if, in the matter of the prisoners, he had thought to do what was best for himself personally (and not what was best for the country) or if he had wanted to remain at home—that such decisions are not "expedient," but are disgraceful, contemptible and morally corrupt.

XXXIII. [116] Our fourth category still remains. It includes decorum, moderation, modesty, continence, and temperance. Is it possible for anything to be expedient that may be contrary to such an ensemble of virtues? The Cyrenaic followers of Aristippus, and the philosophers declaring adherence to the name of Anniceris[255]

---

[254] Caius Acilius (fl.155 B.C.) was a senator and historian, who wrote a lost history of Rome in Greek.

[255] Anniceris was a Cyrenaic philosopher who flourished around 300 B.C. According to Diogenes Laertius (II.86) he ransomed Plato. Aristippus of Cyrene (c.435—356 B.C.) was the founder of the Cyrenaic school. The chief feature of the Cyrenaics was their emphasis on physical pleasure. But this aspect of their philosophy has been exaggerated or misunderstood; they were not hedonists, but advocated a life of balance and moderation. *See* Diogenes Laertius II.86-88 for a short summary of Aristippus's doctrines.

considered everything good to be found in physical pleasures. They considered that virtue should be praised only insofar as it is able to generate voluptuary satisfaction. These schools have become obsolete, but Epicurus flourishes in our own day and he is a proponent and spokesman for basically the same creed. Combat "with infantry and cavalry," as the saying goes, must be waged against this doctrine, if one is to protect and preserve his sense of moral goodness.

[117] For if (as Metrodorus has written)[256] not only expediency, but also a good life, are sustained completely by a healthy physical constitution and the prospect that this will continue, then certainly this expediency (and indeed the highest expediency as people see it) will run into conflicts with moral rectitude. Firstly, where will we give a place for prudence in this situation? Would its position be to collect physical charms from various sources? How wretched this would be for fettered virtue, to be subservient to physical pleasures!

And what would be the duty of wisdom? To collate physical pleasures intelligently? Nothing may be more enjoyable than to do this, but can you imagine anything more decadent? If someone says that pain is the greatest evil, what importance does he attach to fortitude, which is defined as contempt for pain and labor? Although in many passages Epicurus writes bravely about enduring pain, we must consider not what he says, but rather what is logically consistent for someone who believes that "the good" is found within the realm of physical pleasure and "the bad" within the realm of pain.

And if I hear him out, he does say much about continence and temperance in various chapters. But, as the saying goes, "the

---

[256] Metrodorus of Lampsacus (c.331—278 B.C.) was a well-known disciple of Epicurus.

water doesn't run."[257] How is it possible for a man to praise temperance, when he places the highest good in bodily pleasures? Temperance is the enemy of the desires, and the desires are the enablers of libidinous indulgence.

[118] When it comes to these three kinds of virtue, people bob and weave with as much adroitness as they can muster. They adopt prudence as that knowledge which supplies enjoyment and wards off pain. They also make use of fortitude in some way; they employ it as a method for banishing fear of death and for enduring pain. They also introduce temperance into this scheme, not easily, but as far as they can; and they say that the magnitude of a pleasure is determined by the absence of pain.

Justice staggers around in a weak condition or, rather, already is sprawled on the ground.[258] The same is true with all those virtues that are found in social intercourse and in human society in general. For neither moral excellence, nor kindness, nor generosity, nor even friendship can exist, if these qualities are not aspired to for their own sake, but are instead valued for the sake of physical pleasure or selfish amusement.

[119] Let us now try, in some way, to bring these concepts together. We have demonstrated that *any expediency that is contrary to moral goodness is no expediency at all*. Similarly, we maintain that *all carnal pleasures are contrary to moral goodness*. In my judgment, Calliphon and Dinomachus are more deserving of blame; they thought they could resolve the controversy by uniting physical pleasure with moral goodness.[259]

---

[257] Literally *aqua haeret* or "the water stops." The image is that the flow of ideas ("water") is obstructed and nothing is moving forward.

[258] I.e., these arguments harm justice and leave her mortally wounded on the ground.

[259] Calliphon was a Peripatetic philosopher of the 2nd century B.C. Dinomachus must have been one of his contemporaries. Both are mentioned in *De*

And this is much like attaching a farm animal to a man. Moral goodness is not suited for such a joining; it rejects it and is repelled by it. The highest good, which ought to be pure, cannot be linked together or adulterated with dissimilar things. But I have written much on this subject in another place, for it is a large topic.[260] Let us now move to our objective.

[120] We have sufficiently discussed how one can adjudicate a situation created when something that appears to be expedient conflicts with moral goodness. And if, however, physical pleasure seems to have the outward appearance of expediency, there can still be no possible conjunction of it with moral goodness. Now, to give physical pleasure its proper due, we can say that it provides a certain zest to our lives that is not insignificant; but it does not provide anything expedient.

[121] You now have, my son Marcus, a gift from your father and the product of much thought on my part. But its worth to you will depend on what use you make of it. These three books must be received as "extra guests" to supplement your notes from Cratippus's teachings. If I had come to Athens (this would have happened, had not my country recalled me home in the middle of my journey there), you might also have heard me speak there. And because my voice speaks to you directly in these volumes, you may devote to them as much time as you can, and as much as you want. When I see that you derive some pleasure out of this branch of philosophy, I hope to speak to you soon in person; but while you are away from home, I will speak to you from a distance.

Goodbye, my young Cicero. Know that you are the most precious thing to me; but you would be even dearer if you could derive some enjoyment from the principles and advice contained here.

---

finibus (V.8.21) as committing the error of trying to blend virtue and physical pleasure.

[260] In his treatise *De finibus*, in book II.

COMMENTARY ON BOOK III

The third book of *On Duties* represents the culmination of Cicero's arguments from the first two books. It perhaps constitutes the fullest expression of his ethical philosophy that we find anywhere in his writings. It also has great practical significance, as it deals with the subject of conflicts: that is, how to resolve situations where moral goodness clashes with expediency. Conflicts are the most common type of moral problem that a person faces. As Cicero sees it, there is a need for a set of "rules" to cope with ethical conflict scenarios (III.4).

He begins by reviewing the opinions of others with regard to ethical conflicts (III.3) and this leads him to the Stoic view of "medium duties." Moral goodness, he again reminds us, is the only true good. As noted in books I and II, Cicero is careful to base this idea on the laws of Nature and on the values of human society (III.4—5). Nothing can be considered advantageous that is not also morally good, even if things appear to be otherwise in the short term. To illustrate this point, Cicero introduces the compelling fable of the "ring of Gyges." Even if it seems that we can get away with immoral behavior, he tells us, there is always a price to be paid. Nature despises moral corruption and will find ways of exacting a price for such conduct (III.8).

Practical matters of law, politics and commerce are taken up in III.11—18. In III.11, Cicero shows himself wise in the ways of political power by noting that a leader's cruelty is generally counter-productive. The would-be dictator can never enjoy a moment's rest, and usually is consumed by the culture of violence that he has created. Cicero then surprisingly shifts gears and explores the rules regarding commercial transactions.

What are the respective duties of buyers and sellers? Even in the modern world, when uniform codes of commercial transactions have been adopted, these questions never lose their relevance. After discussing fraud and defalcation, Cicero enunciates a concept that has become a cornerstone of modern law: good faith (III.17). For commerce to run smoothly and for the court systems to run efficiently, good faith must be embraced by all. Bad faith—that is, not playing by the rules of honesty or decorum—is not only "against wisdom," it is against Nature herself (III.17). Those who deliberately misrepresent material things to others violate their obligations to their fellow men.

We do not expect the wealth of practical commercial and legal issues that Cicero gives us in book III. But they are certainly welcome. For a work of ethical philosophy, *On Duties* is refreshingly free of tortuous Aristotelian definitions, categories and epistemological spider webs. Instead, we get discussions on real estate transactions, grain merchants, contract law, estate planning, wills and other practical topics. The common theme running through all these discussions is the emphasis on the need for good faith in dealings with others. The temporary material gain we might achieve from greed is never worth it. This point is made strikingly well in the story of Gratidianus (III.20): small violations can carry serious consequences. Any expediency we seek must always be grounded in moral rectitude (III.21); Pompey and Caesar both forgot this and were thus led to ruin (III.21).

Cicero shifts gears a bit in chapter twenty-two with his imaginary dialogue between Diogenes and Antipater. Sometimes, no matter how hard we try to escape the choice, we may be faced with picking the least of two evils (III.28). He takes a swipe at the Epicureans in III.29 and III.33 when he reminds us that moral corruption, and not physical pain, is the greatest evil. Moral rightness can never be based on pleasure, the avoidance of pain, or on personal advantage. Cicero strongly opposes this view. Even though the Epicureans pay lip service to the idea of enduring hardship with dignity, it is impossible for them to reconcile this position with their doctrine that pleasure is the highest good. While physical pleasure can provide some spice for our lives, he admits, it cannot form a basis for moral goodness. With his final affectionate comments to his son Marcus, Cicero brings his treatise to an end.

INDEX

A

B

C

230

231

233

41799597R00133

Made in the USA
San Bernardino, CA
21 November 2016